HOW SHALL WE FIND THE FATHER?

HOW SHALL WE FIND THE FATHER?

Meditations for Mixed Voices

MARY NEILL

DON BRIEL

RONDA CHERVIN

The Seabury Press / New York

1983
The Seabury Press
815 Second Avenue
New York, N.Y. 10017

Printed in the United States of America.

Library of Congress Cataloging in Publication Data:
Neill, Mary.
 How shall we find the Father?
1. Lord's prayer—Meditations. I. Briel, Don.
II. Chervin, Ronda. III. Title.
BV230.N36   1983   242'.5   83-4745
ISBN 0-8164-2623-6

All biblical references are to the Revised Standard Version of the Bible: Old
Testament Section, copyright © 1952; New Testament Section First Edition,
copyright © 1946; Second Edition © 1971 by Division of Christian Education of
the National Council of Churches of Christ in the United States of America.

Acknowledgments:
From *The Kabir Book* by Robert Bly. Copyright © 1971 by Robert Bly. Re-
printed by permission of Beacon Press.
Rainer Maria Rilke, *The Book of Hours*. Copyright 1941 by New Directions
Publishing Corporation. Reprinted by permission of New Directions.
From Maria von Franz, *The Passion of Perpetua*, copyright 1949 by Spring Pub-
lications. Reprinted by permission of the publisher.
An excerpt from "Strung Memories" by Sr. Maria Jose Hobday, in *Parabola*,
Volume 4, #4, page 5, is used with permission of the publisher.

"And which of us shall find his father
know his face and in what place
and in what time
and in what land?"
Thomas Wolfe

". . . there find a father whom we have
never met . . . who has lived since, longing
for his child whom he saw only once.
When you light a lamp you will see him."
Robert Bly

Sing aloud, O daughter of Zion;
Shout, O Israel!
Rejoice and exult with all your heart . . .
The King of Israel, the Lord, is in your midst . . .
He will rejoice over you . . .
He will renew you in his love;
He will exult over you with loud singing
As on a day of festival.
Zephaniah 3: 14–17

Contents

Who Are We?

I, Mary Neill, am a Dominican sister of the Congregation of San Rafael, California. I am assistant professor of religious studies at the University of San Francisco, where I teach undergraduate studies in the winter session and the comprehensive seminar for the master's program in spirituality in the summer session. I give workshops in journal keeping and various other topics relating to religion and psychology under the aegis of Inscape Explorations, of which I am co-director. Other books coauthored with Ronda Chervin include *The Woman's Tale* and *Bringing the Mother with You*, both published by Seabury Press.

I, Don Briel, am a husband and father of four. I have a doctorate in theology from the University of Strasbourg, France. I am currently an assistant professor of theology at the College of St. Thomas, St. Paul, Minnesota.

I, Ronda Chervin, am a wife and mother of three, a Jewish convert to the Catholic faith. I am a professor of philosophy at Loyola Marymount University of Los Angeles. Books I have written include *The Church of Love, The Art of Choosing, The Prayer and Your Everyday Life Series*, and the books coauthored with Mary Neill. I lecture and give workshops and retreats throughout the United States.

1

Preface

This book is the third in a series of coauthored meditation work-books. The first dealt with our inner orphaned child as revealed in fairy tales: *The Woman's Tale*; the second, *Bringing the Mother with You*, touched on using the rosary in one's search for nurturing consciousness. This third book, to which we two women invited a third, male voice, honors the quest for the father, using the petitions of the Our Father to crystallize our understanding of all that "fathering" can mean. "For this reason I bow my knees before the Father, from whom every family in heaven and on earth is named." (Eph. 3:14-15).

One of the reviewers of our last book thought we had actually written two separate books, but thinly joined. And lest you have the impression that you will find here now three distinct books, three separate voices, it seems important to explain our vision and process. (One writer noted that he always listened to critics and then did precisely that for which he was chided, since it was sure to focus on his uniqueness.)

First, this book needs to be read slowly and meditatively, with time for written or verbal response. It is the task of the reader to help weave the connections between the opposites s(he) will find so clearly voiced on these pages. Spiritual synthesis, which tries to weave the conceptual and affective, requires interiority. This is, as it were, a meditation workbook.

The unevenness in our book is in a sense deliberate; we emphasize our separate and distinct voices and styles so that you may have the courage to articulate yours, however raw and unfinished it emerges. We write to teach ourselves and you. Our method is part of the teaching and demands patience with the "jarring" of separate selves, the meandering passageways, the gaps within and without. Enough readers have shared with us that working through the material in written or shared form has been liberating for them that we were encouraged to continue this approach.

Each of us, however painful it is to acknowledge or however much we wish it otherwise, lives in an isolated consciousness, a peculiar monad never before seen or experienced. We tap on our fortressed prisons, and occasionally someone taps back and we are delivered through imagination, longing, and faith from our isolation for that time of meeting. Then we swirl back into that island consciousness, living by faith that there is a firmament below under the waters of separation which connects us, or we could never have imagined the possibility of meeting in the first place.

It is when, through your reflections on these pages, you touch the firmament below within yourselves that your connectedness — our connectedness — will emerge. The aloneness of the mature Christian is not delivered into a fusion of style and voice but into an inclusion that honors separateness. It is a Western vision of God that we, unlike followers of Eastern religions, hope not to be fused with God, but to see Him face to face in the beatific vision. "Now I see darkly as in a mirror, then I shall see as I am seen," Paul writes to the Corinthians.

We hope in our writing to pass on to you not smoothly articulated thoughts, but something of our self-being as it struggles to acknowledge its "fathering forth" from God and its power to father forth life in others by saying yes to each person's unique goodness and ambiguity.

4

Sent forth from the natural domain of species into the hazard of the solitary category, surrounded by the air of a chaos which came into being with him, secretly and bashfully he watches for a Yes which allows him to be, and which can come to him only from one human person to another. It is from one man to another that the heavenly bread of self-being is passed.

(Martin Buber, *The Knowledge of Man*, p. 71)

Why Do We Write This Book?

Why Do I Write This Book?

MARY NEILL

† When I came home from Switzerland where I had been on a sabbatical and walked into my parents' home, I found that my dad had set the kitchen clock to Swiss time so that during the months I was away they could know—he could know—the time wherever I was. I was deeply moved by this gesture.

And for at least three years or more, I have kept on my bulletin board a quotation from Thomas Wolfe. (It is written on the back of a "Happy Mother's Day" card.) "And which of us shall find his father, and know his face and in what place, and in what time, and in what land?" My unconscious knew I was searching for a deeper understanding of fathers long before I did. The parallel notion that fathers are searching for their children for me has been gift, grace, revelation.

Recently, at a poetry reading by Robert Bly, when he spoke of his own father and all the fathers of our times, tears flowed down my face and I knew that the search for the father is not just my solitary task but that of all of us. And I knew for the first time, too, that the Father—and the fathers—search too for the child.

Bly's thought was that five minutes after each child is born, the father loses her/him, for in our time the values of the home are those of the mother. Bly pictures the father as living thereafter "longing for his child whom he saw only once. . . . When you light the lamp," he says, "you will see him—the father you have never met."

So this book is partly to light the lamp and see more clearly my father, all fathers, the Heavenly Father, that Prodigal whom Jesus described as running out to greet the child who had thrown everything away.

We live in a time of anger at the fathers. I have felt that often in myself and for a long time was afraid of enraged feminists who would return to matriarchy, who insisted that our world would "wan and piecemeal lie" until we said not "God bless you," but "goddess bless you." "It is the fathers who have oppressed us, stolen our birthright," they cry, and they are not totally wrong—nor are they totally right, either.

How can I become free by hating the other, I wonder? How can I hate, when there is no other? When I am father, too, and my sins are his, and his mine? How shall I come to the mind that was in Christ Jesus, the religious consciousness I hope to touch upon in order to empty myself of prejudices and fears—old wounds—and to purify my vision until I can see something of what Jesus saw in the Father's face, that something that strengthened His power to love and suffer, to see all children as God's children.

I write, too, because this book has grown somehow out of the first book, The Woman's Tale, which dealt with the archetypal child lost in the woods, and the second, Bringing the Mother with You, which dealt with the mother we must bring with us. Now, with the third, we consider the father who helps give form to life.

I feel that for me, and for many in our times, until we struggle with our beginnings, our trinitarian nature, we cannot move to the fourth thing, the heavenly Jerusalem, where the grief of the abandoned child, the deserted woman, and the isolated father will be wiped away.

For Personal Reflection

1. What clues from your consciousness and unconscious life reveal the father quest to you? What poems, songs, quotations move you (such as the lines of Robert Bly or Thomas Wolfe)?
2. When you are searching for someone, do you have difficulty believing that what you search for is searching for you? When in your life have you recognized you are not the only one searching? That someone is on the other end?
3. How do you feel about women enraged at the "sins of the fathers," which have set their teeth on edge? Can you accept the idea of God as father?
4. The "father consciousness" serves to give form, to set limits. What energies of yours too easily dissipate because they have no form? Where do you have the most difficulty setting limits and boundaries?

Why Do I Write This Book?

DON BRIEL

In a recent issue of *The New Yorker* a young man described the moment of the birth of his first child. At the instant of his son's birth, the man glanced out the window at the frenzied movement of the urban landscape. But for him, out of the confusion there was "an eternal moment: dazzling clarity." These are moments that call from us the name *sacred*, and they are marked off from our profane existence precisely because we experience them as gift. It is in this way that one first experiences fatherhood, as gift which allows participation in an eternal order of meaning and clarity. As T. S. Eliot has said, it is at the still point that there is the dance.

Surely this is one reason for a relatively new desire to capture the moment of birth on film, so that it can be available to us again in the future. But this may betray the reality itself, for films tend merely to invite a passive review of these sacred moments, leaving the viewer unable to recreate them actively. This is not merely the stuff of photograph albums; it partakes of a larger dimension of human life: the need to allow our consciousness to open itself to the experience of fatherhood in order that we may realign our sense of the real.

Such moments are themselves transitory and sporadic. Our lives are bounded by the familiar tangle of unfocused events and emotions which seem to demand our ordering. But those moments that touch the eternal liberate us from a merely functional understanding of our identity. To be a father is not merely to act out a role; it has something to do with being itself, it is part of a larger reality.

We tend to occupy ourselves with functional evaluations of fatherhood. It seems clear to us that the "father knows best" model is no longer acceptable. But it is also clear that recent Hallmark commercials, which suggest that fatherhood might best be expressed by the figure of a hapless tongue-tied man purchasing a meaningful card for his daughter's sixteenth birthday because he can express his affection in no other way, are equally distortions of the reality.

The Hallmark image is more appreciated in our own time because it suggests that understanding fatherhood has more to do with a child's ability to perceive a generally good will which is ineptly expressed than with a recognition of a man's active participation in the life of his child. This newer image of fatherhood stresses a passive element. We have ceased to understand a father's function and so seek to grasp our relationship to him on a more basic level. We tend now not so much to define our fathers by what they do for us, but by what they are to us. We stress not their distinctive activities in our lives, but a presence to us which links us to the past.

No longer do films emphasize the strong guiding hand of the father, shaping the developing aspirations of his child. Rather, the contemporary father figure is that of the man who has been separated from his child for many years and has just recently, probably accidentally, been encountered.

It is a mistake to think that the preoccupation with this phenomenon of the displaced father serves to reduce fatherhood to a mere biological reality. In fact, it marks a continuing fascination with the idea of fatherhood as being something more than simply a functional reality. We seek reassurance of the existential reality of our relatedness to our father.

A man is a father not primarily because he acts like a father, but because he participates in some sort of larger reality and therefore gives us a place in a cosmic order of meaning. A father is important because our relationship to him is central in defining who we are as persons.

This is not to deny that a man's willingness to involve himself in the unsettling world of diapers, teething, flu, and braces has to do with the process of becoming a father, but it is clear that the recent emphasis on equality of sexual roles has produced a renewed interest in defining the essential qualities of fatherhood and motherhood. As functions grow more and more similar, we have a greater need to understand the more basic reality of father and mother.

Surely the great risk for the believer is the tendency to deny in the darkness what he has seen in the light. At the births of my four children, I have experienced moments of clarity like those of the young man from New York. I have felt the gift of life and fatherhood and have known that it marked a participation in the sacred.

This is a sense easily squandered in the convulsive movement to "father" one's children. I sense the need to recover the sacred dimension of fatherhood, both as a father and as a son. Somehow, to call God our Father is to transform ourselves as persons, and we need to understand the nature of the conversion that is implied in hungering for—and even more, in accepting—a father's love.

For Personal Reflection

1. What is your reaction to seeing photographs and films of the birth process? How can this wonder at new life, experienced in an ambiguity of joy and pain, best be expressed?
2. How could one renew this experience of wonder at birth in recalling our participation in it?
3. As a father or as a child, do you find yourself lapsing into losing

the sense of the mystery of paternity in the day-to-day living out of the role?

4. Do you think of paternity more as an active, guiding role, or as a role of passive acceptance? What is the most distinctive gift your father has given you?

Why Do I Write This Book?

RONDA CHERVIN

When I think of God the Father, His image is veiled, distant, yet beckoning. Religious believers speaking of the Father give a tender note to that name. Is the Father, then, a different being from the God of the philosophers, who is the apex of being, creator of the universe, absolute beauty, truth, and goodness?

When I close my eyes and wait for images of fatherliness to come, what I see is homey, sweet, funny. I picture myself as a small cat in the lap of a large man. He is stroking my fur, crooning, "Nice kitty, nice kitty." All is safe. My own father adored animals. For some time he was a zoo keeper. During our childhood there were dogs and cats and even snakes living with us. Perhaps I experienced my father's love most when he looked on me and my sister as his dearest, cutest animals.

When we were eight years old our parents were divorced. There was a break, estrangement, reunion, another long hiatus, then a coming together again. Just prior to the last reencounter, I was sitting in a monastery chapel during a retreat, meditating on the Father without much insight, when suddenly I felt a comforting hand come from deep in the past, rushing forward to my back. The words I heard in my heart were: "I was always with you, my daughter." God the Father was becoming more vivid.

My favorite images of fatherhood came from watching my husband with our children. From the time my twin girls were one-year-olds until they were six, before bed they would perch on my husband's knees while he made up a different story for them every night. They would giggle until their diapers overflowed. It was the best part of the day. The father was the teller of tales, the expander of consciousness beyond the confines of the house into the world of fantasy.

Eight years after the birth of our twins we had a son. He looked exactly like my husband, only fifty-three years younger. As the father gazed at the son with delight and the son at the father with gurgling pleasure, I saw an image of the Father and the Son, and of God and all us children. The Father creates, nourishes, sets free, and then reaps the harvest. Not without suffering. No pain my daughters and son went through did not doubly pierce the heart of their father.

Writing this book may be a bridge for me between the God of the philosophers, the human fathers of my present and past life, and the living God of Scripture. When I address the God of the philosophers I ask Him such questions as "Why did You ever create mankind at all, knowing how we would mess up the world?" To the thinker, man is absurd. When I address the God of the Bible, however, I ask instead, "When will You bring me into Your kingdom? When will I surrender to Your plan with faith and trust?" To the believer man is a funny creature with a terrific destiny.

And so I want to explore the many faces of God the Father. Not to lose the magnificent visage of the metaphysical God, but to blend it with the cozy image, that "my joy may be full." How better than to trace His countenance in the prayer of Jesus—the *Our Father?*

There is one other biblical image which flashed up to provide a theme for my writing. It comes from the book of Zephaniah (3: 14–17). I heard it first as a rousing song by Carey Landry entitled "And the Father Will Dance." It filled me with incredible bliss.

> Shout with joy, daughter of Zion.
> Rejoice, exult with all your heart,
> Yahweh your God is in your midst,
> He will exult with joy over you,
> He will renew you by his love,
> He will dance with shouts of joy for you as on a day of festival.

For Personal Reflection

1. Why are you reading this book?
2. What images does the word *father* call up in your mind?
3. Is there a contrast between your intellectual ideas of God and biblical or experiential images?
4. When have you been most angry at your own father? At God the Father?
5. As you begin to read our book, what feelings are you experiencing?

Chapter 1

Meditations on Our Father Who Art in Heaven

Our Father Who Art in Heaven

MARY NEILL

† Ronda's image of the father as distant and beckoning put me in touch with why, when I try to begin with picturing our Father in heaven, I collapse and must begin with memories and images of our fathers on earth.

That this is not my problem alone but that of our time was illuminated with a discussion of St. Perpetua's dream by a Jungian analyst, Edward Edinger. The dream of the twenty-two-year-old mother, martyred about 100 A.D., is as follows:

> I beheld a ladder of brass of miraculous size which reached up to Heaven and was so narrow that it could only be ascended singly. On either side of the ladder, all manner of iron implements were fastened—swords, lances, hooks, daggers and spears—so that any one who was careless or who did not hold himself erect while climbing was torn to pieces and remained hanging. Beneath the ladder lay a gigantic dragon, lying in wait for the climbers and frightening them away.

15

Saturus [who converted her] went up before me (just as he later chose to be put to death first, for love of us because it was he who had taught us but afterwards was not with us when we were thrown into prison). And he reached the top of the ladder and turning to me, spake: "Perpetua, I am holding thee, but see that the dragon does not bite thee." And I answered: "He shall not harm me in the name of Jesus Christ." And the dragon slowly lifted his head out from under the ladder, as if in fear of me, and I trod on it, as though I were treading on the first rung of the ladder, and ascended to the top. And I beheld a vast garden and seated in the centre of it, a tall white-haired man, in shepherd's dress, who was milking sheep and round about him many thousands of people clad in white. And he raised his head, looked at me, and spake: "It is well that thou are come, child." And he called me to him and gave me also a morsel of the cheese which he was milking and I received it with folded hands and ate. And all who stood around said, "Amen." And at the word of this invocation I awoke, and was aware that I was still eating something sweet, I know not what. And I immediately reported the vision to my brother and we understood that it meant the coming passion. And from that time we began to put no more hope in this world.[1]

I was amazingly moved by the last line: "And . . . [they placed] no more hope in this world." Edinger believes that this was what he calls an "over-arching dream," one that expressed the task of the collective for over a thousand years: to leave the earthiness of the Roman culture—its entombment in material things, roads, aqueducts, empires—and to sublimate matter's energy into something invisible. Spiritual life is about ladders and sublimation, Edinger notes. He also holds the opinion that our age's spiritual problem is too many ladders, too much abstraction, too much flying away. Many who come to him for therapy, he notes, need first to be grounded in their lives before they can begin genuine sublimating. His insight made great sense to me. I had wondered why so many summer courses at the University of San Francisco concern spirituality or sexuality. "Was Solomon, who had a thousand wives, sexual or spiritual?" the mystic Rumi asks—and so do we.

I have thought about the dream a lot, and it occurs to me that the spiritual step of our time is more complicated that it was for Perpetua. We must step down, be grounded, before we may climb to see the Father in the field at the top of the ladder. (How touching to me the details of her dream: the white haired man calling her "child," milking sheep, giving her sweet cheese.) No wonder we search for the man Jesus. "Were you really human?" We ask. "Did you come down—were you real? Flesh?"

I have found myself in teaching theology convinced that first I must ground the students in their own lived questions, the revelations that their lives contain, before I can speak of heavenly things. Bankrupt of earth, with no place to stand, how can we hope to touch the sky? Sometimes I am mockingly accused of teaching "touchy—feely" courses, and that is not entirely wrong. To my students I say, "Feel and taste your own lives—only then might you possibly feel your need for God."

And I often end the course by telling them of Perpetua's dream and the need for one of them to have a dream for our time, a dream that causes them, upon awakening, to turn to their brother or sister and say, "Now because of this dream, let us begin to put more hope in this world." For surely that is the spiritual task of our time: How shall we find images that cause us to place hope in this torn, apocalyptic world? In becoming man, God placed hope in this world and named that hope Jesus—so we must do as our Heavenly Father and enmesh ourselves in our world, calling that hope by our own name in Christ.

And so, to reach my Heavenly Father, I, a child of my fly-away age, will touch with you the images of my earthly fathers, briefly naming the gift they fathered in me.

My own sweet father gave me life. A Japanese master said at a lecture once: "Why are you Americans so mad at your parents? We Japanese honor them because they called us from infinity that we might make our way back there." The more I obey my call back home to infinity, the more I can be grateful centrally that my father gave me life itself. And he gave me so much more: warmth and affection (how easily he cried); the memories of his praying beside me in church; always money to get myself a treat; spiced tea and a heavy overcoat mailed to Europe (all to keep me warm); the memory of a man working with gnarled hands painting signs and doing it well; a man building his own houses; a man who stopped always to help the stranger and alone, bringing them home for warmth and food. It was a shock to me when I entered the convent and found that everyone does not stop and help those with car trouble. There are memories of a man who knew how to ask forgiveness, a humble man. "Pappy," his friends around Bethel Island called him, and they gave him a cake last Father's Day. They knew the sweetness of him — not just Father or Daddy, but Pappy too.

Another father image comes from my grandad Ross, who taught me how to play gin rummy with him when I was four and bought me a pair of red cowboy boots. A little girl given red boots and the knowledge of cards is going to make it.

My grandad Neill, very faintly known in fact, was honored as the Texas Ranger, the pioneer, part of the family that fought and won the Texas war for independence. "Remember the Alamo" runs in my blood, and so does revolution. A great gift for living amidst wars.

Father Joe Servente, who taught us Augustine and Thomas in the novitiate, opened the *Summa* and taught me that theology was handmaiden to the Songs of Songs, Aquinas's favorite scripture, read to him while he lay dying. Father Servente taught me that theology at its best was love made thought, that it loved all the objections, incorporated the tradition, and left you ready to praise God. Father Servente died at thirty-seven saying, "My God, I love you." I'm grateful to him for a vision of the *Summa* that no narrow neo-scholastic has been able to destroy for me.

From high school years come memories of tough old Monsignor McGough, the last of the feudal Irish warlords in Stockton, who paid me well to help with his mailing list and drove me home, cursing and shouting at the other drivers on the road — and he in his Roman collar. I was appalled at the time and later glad that he gave me the gift of knowing that being real is more important than

18

looking holy. He would scare us witless in school assemblies, cutting to size some destructive and smart-aleck kid. We trembled for the delinquent but were glad for the father who would set the limit to destructive behaviors: "I will not tolerate destruction," he would shout. Where have the fathers gone who can contain our destructive children?

One of my former students, Don Briel, longtime friend, our co-author, has fathered much in me: a love of France—"Go there to study," he said, "it will change your life." And it did! He gave me Maritain and Mauriac, Merton every year, Beatles' songs and Lisa Minelli movies, a respect for the tradition and suspicion of the merely novel—and so much more. Perhaps most deeply, a passageway to my lost, introverted self.

Two men in Europe fathered forth the philosopher and theologian in me. The British philosopher John Macmurray sent the only extant copy of his bibliography when I was doing my doctoral dissertation on his religious thought. He welcomed me with warmth and openness and sent loving letters across the oceans and years.

My director in Strasbourg, Maurice Nedoncelle, confirmed my writing, my thought, my style and explained the heart of Frenchness to me in one electric scene: "Your English style is fine; the French translation falters. If no one in the whole world reads the French version but myself and the two other jury members, the French language must be respected." He polished parts of my thesis himself, willing to suffer for the French language. I was amazed to see such love of language—I had never thought to suffer for English. I keep his Christmas letters, magi gifts of gold, and when he died I sorely missed him. That two eminent European scholars believed in my work and my person protected me in many a sterile academic storm that I later encountered. Their welding of love and thought in their personalities and relationships calls me to live in their image.

Father Al Zabala, head of the theology department at the University of San Francisco, gave me the gift of believing in myself as teacher, theologian, religious woman. He protected me when I was once attacked by an irate parent. "Mary Neill's like Jesus," he said, "the students love her or sometimes hate her." What a wonderful defense. Al's vision of what a theology department could be, its strength in bearing conflict and the tension of many opposite personalities, has been a strong support.

Closer to my home and family, I love to see my nephews, young fathers in their thirties, play with their children. Bob teases Tara, and she is princess of his delights. Pete puts his hand on three-year-old Justin's shoulder and calls him "son," and the word is a sacrament as he says it. "You can play outside near me while I work, son," he says, and Justin knows he is a prince—his father's heir.

The last image of a young father that recently charmed me I saw at a picnic near a lake. Some young mothers had left their husbands to watch the babies, all under three. The young men drank, laughed, and talked. One two-year-old kept running about and running away, and the young father would have to go catch him. Finally the father sat down in the chair, put the child flat, and rested his foot on his son's back. No mother would ever do that, I thought, smiling, and yet the child seemed content, pinned by his father from erratic forays. Young fathers throw their children higher in the air, tease them harder, pin them down quicker than mothers, and the children are the better for it. The father's strength seems to give a wider container to wildness and fun. Happy the child whose father has thrown him in the air or pinned him with a loving foot or arm.

As I gather together the abundant earthly father images given me, I use them to imagine my Heavenly Father. Nedoncelle wrote: "Do not imagine our heavenly father to be less than the fathers of the earth who follow their children with tenderness."

So my Heavenly Father is playful, confirming, searching, limiting, deep and mystical, tender—and mine. He pins me down with foot or arm. He sets heavenly clocks for me so I can know what time it is wherever He is and wherever I am.

Our fathers who are of earth, show us the face of the Heavenly Father, His protective arm and foot, His playful hand and face. Let not my grimness color God laughless and gray. Let me know, as Meister Eckhart knew: "The Father laughs as He brings forth the Son and they laugh and bring forth the Holy Spirit, and they all laugh and bring forth creation."

For Personal Reflection

1. Who are the men who have fathered forth some aspect of your person? Have you thanked them for this gift — in fact or imagination? "Only the grateful praise God," says the poet Kabir.
2. Write out a dream or a fantasy that would cause you to say, "Now I can place some hope in this world."
3. Where in your life do you feel the need for grounding? What occasions cause your energy to evaporate?
4. Write a prayer asking for the qualities you are most searching for in a father — outer, inner or heavenly.

Our Father Who Art in Heaven

DON BRIEL

One of Graham Greene's characters once said that the hardest thing in life is to understand that only God and one's parents, in spite of the fact that they truly know who we are, could truly love us. It isn't accidental that we so often link parents and God.

We see them serving similar functions in our lives although we rarely try to define the similarities with any precision. They are both credited with a vague responsibility for our conception and continuing existence; they are both authority figures, benevolent but too often vindictive; they are both perpetually old in relation to us and rather fragile in that they demand a certain filial reverence and duty. We early learn to suspect the dependence that this demand for respect implies.

In all this we link them and in so much more. But just as we relate parents and God functionally, we also know that maturity has something to do with accepting our parents as persons and not merely defining them by the roles which they have exercised in our lives.

21

This is true for God as well. Maturity implies an escape from the world of the nursery in which all things are reflections of a child's self-image. To say this is not, however, to suggest that their roles are unrelated to their identities. As Hopkins has said in "As Kingfishers," ". . . the just man justices; / Keeps grace that keeps his goings graces; / Acts in God's eye what in God's eye he is, —Christ —for Christ stays in ten thousand places, / Lovely in limbs, and lovely in eyes not his / To the Father through the features of men's faces."

In the past, to call a man a father was to say something central about him as a person, and we sense that the same thing is true when we call God our Father. We use the term as a metaphor, but that is not to lessen its importance or undermine its implications.

The problem, however, remains. In our own age the term father seems to have a merely sentimental significance. We have lost any sense of the vital reality which the term once connoted. Tillich noted this phenomenon some thirty years ago: "The fatherhood of God, which is the greatest and most incredible concept of Christianity, has become one of the most usual and insignificant phrases of daily life."[2]

For most Christians a willingness to "dare" to call God our Father is simply conventional, performed without any sense that in referring to God as Father we are saying anything central about him as a person. The same thing is true on the purely human level.

In the New Testament, Christ often compares God to a human father, and in the comparison we know that something important about God is revealed; but we cannot begin to grasp the significance of the comparison unless we attempt to rediscover what is important about fatherhood in the first place. One thing is certain: these Scriptural comparisons always have to do with the love of a father.

I had always thought that being a father would be the most natural of tasks, simply allowing a free expression of oneself, of one's love for his children. I thought it would be a direct and uncomplicated affair, and I was always confused by the realization that it was far from simple and uncomplicated for my own father. I knew his anguish and disappointment. I knew that fatherhood was not for him an essentially joyful reality. It was sometimes more like a trial. It was hard on him. But I felt not bound by his blood, and I looked forward to storing up a hoard of knowledge and wisdom and experience in order to make these available to my own children in Godlike benevolence and independence.

The reality of fatherhood has been different, of course, and I have often been struck by the fact that what fathers and God may truly have in common is a love which is more accurately characterized by dependence than by independence. Both God and fathers offer themselves, pledge themselves to their children; but their children are in no way bound to respond in kind. In fact, the reverse is true.

Fatherhood isn't easy. So it is in the story of the Prodigal Son; we sense the father's dependence, the son's independence. The significance of the son's return to the father and its difficulty can be understood in the light of Graham Greene's insight into a certain human ambivalence about parental and divine love.

The Prodigal Son rejected his father's love because he sensed that to accept the fact that he was loved for what he truly was would be to accept the fact that he could not become anything he wished to be. He looked instead to be loved by those who might be dazzled by his varied masks. We forget how much like the Prodigal Son we really are. The resemblance may have less to do with our shared hunger for fleshpots and general decadence than it does with a shared tendency to resist our parents, to resist God, which involves clinging to the illusion that all things are possible for us.

To accept that we are loved for what we truly are is to accept our being, our rootedness in a larger reality. In this sense, to accept a father's love is to accept a place within a tradition and to admit that one's identity as a person is not principally a private reality at all, but has to do with relatedness. The Prodigal Son was led to redefine himself by accepting his relatedness to his father. We tend to think of his return as marking a mere restoration of the earlier relationship, the son's submission allowing a resumption of things as they were. Actually the return of the son marked a transformation.

The son was not the same, nor was the father, and the jealous brother knew it perhaps better than anyone else. The Prodigal Son had left his father's house because he could not bear the burden of being loved. He felt only the confinement of his father's affection. He experienced love passively and keenly felt its demand.

He returned to his father in dependence, having learned to love. He returned, however, not to accept his father's definition but to accept the relatedness in which his identity might be realized. This is the point of the story of the Prodigal Son.

Kierkegaard said that the acceptance of our identity grounds us in the sacred, and so, as John Dunne pointed out, Kierkegaard's faith "consisted of facing this dreadful thing, his own individuality, and accepting it, like St. Francis of Assisi kissing the leper. Each man had a leper to kiss, we might say, but the leper was not another person as it was for Francis; it was himself in his own individuality."[3]

It is in his engagement with his father that the Prodigal Son kissed the leper and discovered what it means to be freed to self-acceptance. So too did the father. What resulted was a quality of tension that freed both men, allowing them to develop the interdependent character of their relationship, and their identities. This was a dynamic and not a static reality.

D. H. Lawrence reminded us, it is paradoxically true that genuine freedom has to do with restricting our horizons of action rather than with expanding them. To accept a father's love is to run the risk, as the Prodigal Son knew, of feeding the pigs. A reversal of values is implied here; the value of things is dependent on the context in which they occur.

To accept a father means that we accept a religious homeland with defined boundaries. It suggests an acceptance of our past and an admission of a kind of continuity into the future. To accept a father is to limit the boundaries of our lives, of our identities, but it offers the possibility of life itself.

The interdependence of a father and his child has begun to suggest to me the fundamentally dialectical character of their relationship. In one sense we father our children insofar as we allow them to father us. The willingness to allow ourselves to be loved and transformed by our children may be central to our children's capacity to accept our love for them, to accept that they are lovable.

As St. Paul has told us, we are called to put on Christ, not to put on the Father. We father our children by reminding them of our mutual sonship, our mutual dependence before God and before each other. Fathers are most comfortable when playing with their children, for they recognize that their relationship is in one sense more fraternal than paternal.

We look to one Father, and those of us who live the role recognize with a certain dread that we do so only as surrogates. To act as a father is to live Christ, to reveal the Heavenly Father to our children.

This is not to minimize the complexity and difficulty of fatherhood, nor does it remove the burden of exercising parental authority, but it does mean that the importance of fatherhood may be principally symbolic. We do not function autonomously but point to the reality of the love of the Father.

To say that the Father is in heaven is to locate Him, to recognize that He is other than human, that He is transcendent. But at the same time, to locate the Father in heaven is to recognize that our home is with Him and that we are thus called to participate in the sacred.

To call God our Father is to accept the curious ambiguity of the human condition in which we find ourselves, as Shakespeare said, crawling somewhere between heaven and earth.

We wish our lives simpler. To accept the Father's love is to accept a religious homeland in which we are called to realize the fullness of our existence, to resolve the paradox in living out its conditions. This is not to settle into a complacent dependency but, like the Prodigal Son, to open ourselves to the relatedness in which we come to self-realization, in which we allow ourselves to be transformed in the Father's image.

For Personal Reflection

1. In what ways do you see your father as fragile or needy? In what ways God? Can you write a prayer reflecting this sense of God?
2. Was fatherhood essentially joyful or disappointing for your father? For you, if you are a father? Do you see God the Father as essentially happy with you or disappointed?
3. Do you reject human or divine love for fear of being trapped in boundaries you have not chosen, preferring the love of those you can "dazzle with your masks"?
4. Can you see kissing the leper of your own identity as related to accepting your father and God?
5. If you are a father, when have you seen yourself as brother to your children, with God as the real father?

Our Father Who Art in Heaven

RONDA CHERVIN

Many times a day I pray these words. They have become an inner song so full of meaning below the level of consciousness that it seems impossible to articulate its meaning without loss. Still I come back to Augustine's famous thought: "What saith any man when he speaks of Thee? Yet woe to them that keep silence, seeing that even they who say most are as the dumb" (Confessions).

I will divide my meditation: first *Our* Father, then *Father*, then *Who Art in Heaven*.

"Our" has a particular resonance for a twin. (I am also a twin as well as a mother of twins.) We never said *my* mother or *my* father, only *our* mother, *our* father. A twin is "with" from the womb onward and always sees the "we" as most natural. I converted to the Church amidst a close community of lay Catholics. Unlike so many of the fifties and sixties who led a somewhat individual religious life, their deepest experiences of God being when alone in a chapel, the Church for my group was always "our Church." But life separated me from my first group of friends. Married to a non-Catholic, my prayer life became more and more introverted. I preferred it when I found a daily Mass with few in attendance. Then I could more readily pretend I was a hermitess!

It was only in entering the charismatic movement years later that I recovered the "we" experience of God. The simple songs of the people of this movement are filled with the sense of creatureliness, need, and above all trust in a God whose first title is Father of the People. Prophecies begin typically with the words "Oh, my children." For me as a philosophy professor, becoming a member of a charismatic prayer community also meant being one of the ordinary people, viewed by them not as an intellectual but as a sister. It often brings tears to my eyes to be one of a crowd of five thousand at a charismatic congress, praising our Father and exulting in His love.

The human image of fatherliness is divided for me between my real father, my godfather, my husband, and other men who have fathered me.

My physical father I associate with two qualities: whimsy and love of beauty. A fiercely independent man, my father was not afraid to give free rein to eccentricity. He taught us to enjoy difference. As preteens bent on achieving popularity through conformity we found our father's caprices a bit embarrassing. He wore brighter clothing than other men. Rather than taking buses or strolling nonchalantly, he would take us on long walking trips through the city of New York, pointing out the scenes, excitedly avid for small and large pieces of beauty. His hobby at that time was playing the kettle drums in a small opera orchestra. At odd moments he would suddenly beat a rhythm on our heads or sing a song loudly.

Meeting him again many years after his departure for the West Coast, I was overwhelmed at the beauty of his house. His appreciation of nature, color, and music shone in the decor, causing me to exclaim with Keats, "'Beauty is truth, truth beauty,'—that is all / Ye know on earth and all ye need to know."

They say rightly that our vision of God the Father is influenced by our experience of our own fathers. It is no accident, then, that I love God especially as Absolute Beauty. I meditate often on His creative genius in the making of all the varied phenomena of the world. I like to laugh with God at His fey humor in making porcupines, skunks, giraffes, hippos, and even the funny shapes and faces of people.

At one time I was aggrieved by the relative ugliness of the human race and questioned God as to why He couldn't make us all look like Botticelli women or Michelangelo men. The answer I thought I heard amused me intensely: Given the fallen nature of man, if everyone were so gorgeous, no one would do anything but ogle each other. He prefers to make us more laughable that we might see the hidden beauty only as a gift flowing from love. Mothers and fathers and lovers see the unique charm; others pass us by and get on with the work of the world.

From my godfather I learned to know goodness, responsibility, and shame. Balduin V. Schwarz, a philosopher and spiritual guide met me as an atheistic graduate student when I was twenty years old. As he shepherded me into the flock of Christ, he witnessed in his person to a fatherly goodness I had not before encountered. Tender care characterized this man's attitudes in all situations. I was particularly impressed by his availability. He was never so busy that he couldn't talk to the stream of visitors and phone callers interrupting his intellectual pursuits. Being a rather wild, self-centered person, I became ashamed as I watched from my vantage point as disciple this man's pure day-by-day goodness.

Finally coming to believe in God the Father,[4] I thought of Him as like my godfather — totally available to me in prayer, trustworthy, but also causing shame as I agonized over the disparity between my new Christian ideals and my abiding selfishness.

Unfortunately life separated me from my beloved godfather and godmother (his wife, also a Jewish convert). They moved back to Europe, from whence they had fled to the United States to escape the Nazis during World War II.

After his departure, the search for the father took many forms in my life. Leaning on my older husband as a father figure, looking for older colleagues and priests became a major part of my emotional pattern for years, changing somewhat for the better when I finally renewed the relationship to my original father. Meeting him again after so many years, I was astounded to learn that he had thought of me and my sister every day of the many years of separation, recalling us as children and longing to see us again. Now when he gazes at me with affectionate joy it gives me deep peace and contentment.

Yet there is still some distrust. My father left us once. He could not protect us. Do I imagine also that God the Father might turn out to be a splendid God, affectionate but not able to protect against ultimate danger from the world, the devil, my own evils?

Of late I have begun to come into a real trust in God, making me less fearful of eventual shipwreck. Connected with viewing myself more as a "funny little creature" than as a "beautiful person with tragic flaws" is a greater sense that my salvation depends on His goodness, not on my merits. As a friend of mine, Fr. Rockwell Shaules, likes to say, "Who do you love better, a little girl with a dirty face, shoelaces untied, who laughs and cries and runs up to strangers, or a big super achiever who gives commands from the vantage point of her high merits?" Spirituality is not like doing push-ups!

I realize that with trust comes comfort, and with this a greater ability to do the good in a peaceful loving way as saints such as Thérèse of Lisieux were able to do. I noticed that my son wraps himself in his afghan in the morning to bring the comfort of his bed into the new day. So should I wrap myself in the cocoon of early prayers of trust so as to move out into the world surrounded by God's love. Images like this one no longer strike me as ridiculously sentimental, for I am recovering my spiritual childhood.

Turning to the words of Jesus "Our Father *who art in heaven*," I think it is very important to make up our minds whether we regard heaven as real or figurative.

One literal interpretation can be found, oddly enough, in the purely philosophical metaphysics of the Hellenic sage Plotinus.

"Let us flee then to the beloved Fatherland. . . . The Fatherland to us is there whence we have come, and there is the Father."[5]

In the Platonic tradition the highest is associated with transcendence, and transcendence with eternity. From our earthly dwelling we glimpse the perfection of truth, beauty, goodness, and love, the temporal manifestations being foretastes of the heavenly experience to come.

But is this heaven a real place as Jesus sometimes seems to imply? Could it not be instead a metaphor for a particularly intense interior experience of God? "The kingdom of heaven is within you."

The way the word heaven is placed in the Our Father prayer, however, seems the clearest indication among many that Jesus thought of God the Father as in another place, called heaven. He could have said, "Our Father who is within you." Even if it is difficult for us to combine the notion of *place* with the metaphysical concept of eternity as being free of space and time, it is impossible to follow Scripture on the basis of heaven being a mere metaphor, unless, of course, we come to view all of the Bible as a vast metaphor for natural life.

For myself as an atheist converted from the despairing view that the universe is meaningless—life a round trip from nothing to nothing—I cherish the idea of the real heaven. I resent those who, eager to make Scripture more understandable to modern man, denude it of its promises, mocking the images the Son uncovered to ground our hope. For me, eternity is the great surprise, the dwelling of the God I had not known before. Sparks of His being dance on earth. He is ever present to His creation. Yes, I affirm the incarnate, immanent God. Yet I long also for heaven as the fulfillment. If God's presence on earth within us was sufficient to fill what Pascal called the God-sized vacuum of man's soul, why would He have needed to send His Son to be crucified for us, to gather up all that was good toward the Parousia?

O Father in heaven
I thank you for the fathers you have sent me.
I thank you for my creation, for my redemption.
I long to see your face —
And the Father will dance!

For Personal Reflection

1. How is your image of God the Father related to your experiences of human fathers in your own life? What wounds in your relationship to your human father might account for difficulties in getting close to God the Father?
2. Do you find God more easily when alone or in a group?
3. How do you picture heaven? How does a clear or fuzzy image of eternity affect your Christian life?

Chapter **2**

Meditations on Hallowed be Thy Name

Hallowed Be Thy Name

MARY NEILL

✝ The archaic flavor of the word "hallow," our inability to replace it with a clearer modern synonym (even if only to avoid the jokes about children who pray "Hollywood be thy name")—these facts point to a gap not just in our language but in ourselves. Language follows life. If the Eskimos have thirty-five words for snow, it is because thirty-five different kinds are real for them. If we use an archaic and vague verb like "hallow," it is because we are so far removed from hallowing, from naming holy, from blessing.

Yet this, the first petition Jesus would have us make to his Father, must be centrally important. May God's name, His presence and power, be praised and acknowledged as holy. "Holy, holy, holy, all the saints adore thee, throwing down their golden crowns beside the glassy sea." This lovely image sung by our ancestors provokes me to ask: When are the times in my life when I have been awed by the holiness in another, in myself, in my experience of God's truth and beauty? What songs of holiness have ever sprung from my lips? What "golden crowns" would I throw down to honor His power and majesty, to divest myself of mine in some fear and trembling? (For some numinous fear characterizes our approach to the holy, Rudolf Otto insists in his book, *The Holy*.) What is the "glassy sea" I must stand beside?

The answers to these questions come hard because perception of, thirst for, longing for holiness are not much discussed or thought of even in religious circles today. When have you looked at someone and thought, How holy? When have you perceived your call from the Lord as simply and centrally a call to holiness? Good works are not enough. The angel in the Book of Revelation praises the Ephesians for their good works, yet chides them: "But I have this against you, that you have abandoned the love you had at first" (Rev. 2:4).

Recently a poem by the mystic Kabir has provoked my meditations:

> I married my Lord, and meant to live with him.
> But I did not live with him, I turned away,
> and all at once my twenties were gone.
>
> The night I was married all my friends sang for me,
> and the rice of pleasure and the rice of pain
> fell on me.
>
> Yet when all those ceremonies were over, I left,
> I did not go home with him,
> and my relatives all the way home said, "It's
>   all right."
>
> Kabir says: Now my love energy is actually mine.
> This time I will take it with me when I go,
> and outside his house I will blow the horn of
>   triumph.
>   (*Poems of Kabir*, translated by Robert Bly)

The poem says it all: the longing of the soul for marriage with the Lord; our easy distraction from that goal, accepted readily by ourselves and our friends ("It's all right"); the readiness for the in-

ner marriage coming only when "my love energy is actually mine";
the ecstacy of release that cries: "I will blow the horn of triumph."
Mystics know of the deep joy and pleasure that holiness, that closeness to the Lord can bring when we are ready to live with him — not
visit, *live*.

The Father is always ready to live with us, for His holy love
energies are always His, always pouring out gifts. "For every good
and perfect gift comes from above, from the Father of light, in
whom there is not shadow or alteration of change." He never fails
in His unconditional love of us; He never curses what He has made.
What "hallowing" means becomes clearer to me when I think of its
opposite, "cursing."

Unlike the Father, how easily we curse. We damn this or that,
oppressed because life and love resist us. Damn family and friends'
expectations; damn the Church and its corruption; damn my weak-
nesses; damn my enemies who mock me; damn the politicians;
damn it that I have lost my friend, my health, my job, my . . .
Damn, damn, damn.

Each of us has a litany of misery, a lamentation song that we
sing, sometimes sadly, sometimes angrily, whose main complaint is
how rotten things are . . . people are . . . how rotten my life is . . . I
am (if we can be so honest). How often have you shuddered when a
friend began his or her misery litany for which you could find no
response? Those who wallow in self-pity, those who hate themselves
for their neurotic wounds and sinfulness should not ignore the
pain, but deepen it so it can be released. Then perhaps they can
move from relentless repetition to the sense that Rilke had when he
wrote: "What is happening in us is worthy of all our love." The
pursuit of holiness is incompatible with self-hatred and cursing.
The next time you feel trapped in misery and self-hatred, try praying, "What is happening in me is worthy of all my love. This is
nothing less than the gate of heaven. God is here and I never knew
it."

"What is happening everywhere is worthy of our love" seems to
me a vision that comes from learning to hallow God's name and
presence. The Father pictured in Genesis delights in all that is.

"And God saw that it was good. . . . and he saw that man was very good." We can only praise God and hallow His name when we can live from a sustained vision of our own goodness and that of all creation. If God is not holy, how can He hear our petitions? If we do not sense, however dimly, our own holiness, how can we pray at all?

"What shall I do not to undo the wonderful works of God in my soul?" Teresa of Avila prayed. And the answer must surely be by hallowing God's name, by owning our capacity for cursing, greed, and ingratitude, which we need to bring to the Lord for transformation in the light of His holiness, by the power of His name into graciousness, joy, and gratitude.

"Be holy" seems a not uncommon exhortation in the Scriptures. Not "feel" holy or "act" holy (in fact there are warnings against such "seeming"). Perhaps a central need of our time is for those of us who, however falteringly, have sensed the holiness of the Lord in ourselves and in others to exhort one another and pray that our thirst for holiness increases; that our love energies may become actually ours; that we may know with deep and effective certitude that we are holy in the image of the Father who is holy. He is whole and undivided in His love, never wavering because we waver, never distrusting because we fail to be trustworthy. We are loved not because we are trustworthy but because we are His. We are holy not through our own power but His. It is our very hollowness resonating with longing for the Lord that is our capacity for holiness. As Kabir says: "When the guest is being sought, it is the intensity of longing that does all the work."

For Personal Reflection

1. List the times in your life when you have felt the call to holiness. Write out one of these memories in detail. What is your present relationship to holiness?
2. What do you feel when (if) someone calls you holy?
3. Describe the holiest person you have met.
4. Meditate on each image of Kabir's poem and write your reaction.

36

5. Write your song of lamentation and cursing, or your misery litany. Feel your capacity for cursing.
6. "Now my love energy is actually mine." When were the moments you have felt the most love energy? What are the obstacles that drain your love energy?

Hallowed Be Thy Name

DON BRIEL

For primitive religious man, the categories of the sacred and the profane marked radically different realities. To identify the sacred, one had only to distinguish it from the profane, from the mass of undifferentiated experience which is the common lot of mankind.

The sacred is the "other than" profane; it is the truly real. In contrast, the profane, in its disorder and fragmentation, seems to be an illusion. Within this perspective, "hallowed be Thy name" serves to emphasize the sacred nature of God and to contrast it with the profane character of the human condition. This posture has an enormous appeal because, as an approach to the real, it has the great advantage of simplicity; moreover, it is a simplicity that is practicable. One can live out the implications of this approach in a relatively direct manner.

One of the reasons that Islam seems to be the fastest growing religion in the world today is that it rests on this central insight: *hasbuna Allah*, "God is our enough." A Muslim is called to worship and submit to the transcendent reality, the wholly otherness of God.

And so, for Islam, there is a truer theological virtue than conviction or understanding; it is deference. The Muslim accepts his radical dependence on God; he rests in his creatureliness. He defers to God, to the other than human.

In the Koran it is written, "To God belong the Excellent Names, so call upon Him by them," but it is important to note the sense in which these names are used. Because God is a fully transcendent, fully sacred reality, one cannot call upon Him with the expectation of a response. So the Muslim finds himself in the curious position of calling upon a nameless reality.

He calls upon Allah because it is his duty to do so and because it demonstrates his dependence in the face of God. God thus remains inviolable. The two most common of these names, the Compassionate and the Merciful, would seem to suggest something of God's essence. Within the framework of Islam, however, nothing specific about God can be deduced from the names themselves, except in the most general sense. God rests in mystery. The two orders of sacred and profane remain distinct and well defined.

The Christian understanding of this phrase, "hallowed be Thy name," cannot be interpreted in such a direct and satisfactory manner. We still reel under the implications of the use of the word "Father." If God is our Father, then the dichotomy of the sacred and profane is in some sense an illusion.

We have much to learn from the humility of Islam, but from the Christian perspective, the Muslim emphasis on submission is incomplete. The radical break between the sacred and profane has been mediated by Christ, and so in a sense we are called to participate in the divine. In the view of the Christian East, we are to become, by grace, what He is by nature.

We do so by imitating Christ. By accepting sonship we give glory to the name of the Father. It is here that we dare to affirm that God is love, and as Christians, we say this in a sense far different from the Muslim affirmation of God's mercy. We do not merely say that God is loving, but that He is love.

To hallow the name of Allah is to submit to His transcendence, to accept our insignificance before His majesty, but how does one hallow the name of the God of love? Again, we can only look to the example of Christ. As Paul reminds us, "he emptied himself to assume the condition of a slave, and became as men are and being as all men are, he was humbler yet, even to accepting death, death on a cross."

Christ gave glory to the Father in his submission to the Father's will, but the life of Christ is of central importance not principally because of his submission but because of what his submission accomplished, the mediation of the sacred and the profane worlds. Christ lived as a servant, and one of the most striking things about his life is the curious link he suggests between service and life itself. In some sense to serve is to live fully.

This is not the submission of the masochist but the fullness of life of the lover. Love is service lived. It is in some sense life itself. The response to the God of love, the hallowing of His name, is life. "It is not only prayer that gives God glory," Hopkins wrote,

> Smiting on an anvil, sawing a beam, whitewashing a wall, driving horses, sweeping, scouring, everything gives God some glory if being in His grace you do it as your duty. To go to communion worthily gives God great glory, but to take food in thankfulness and temperance gives him glory too. To lift up the hands in prayer gives God glory, but a man with a dung-fork in his hand, a woman with a slop-pail, give him glory too. He is so great that all things give him glory if you mean they should. So then, my brethren, live.[6]

To hallow God's name is to live and to live fully. No wonder the Christian is so often aware of a kind of nostalgia for a simpler world in which he was called merely to reverence the sacred. Submission is not enough. The Christian feels called to life. He is called to live the fullness of life given by the Father's love.

This perspective eliminates the traditional distinction between the sacred and the profane. Here the sacred is not alone real, but all things, no matter how profane, mark openings to the sacred. All things are transformed in Christ.

As a result the religious nostalgia for the sacred world, while natural enough in itself, can be seen to be an obstacle to the awareness of the strange relatedness of all things and, more directly, to the terrifying reality of the nature of the Christian task, which is to participate in the sanctification of the world. And so we stare at the slop-pail, at the dung-fork, and ponder the mystery of the Incarnation, the mystery which opens to us the awareness of the Father's love.

This understanding begins to suggest a kind of interdependence between the love of the Father and the loving response of men. If God loves us as a father, is this not limiting His inviolability, does it not imply that He is, in some obscure way, dependent on the love of His children as are other fathers?

Characteristically, Rilke asks the unaskable question "What will you do, God, when I die? / When I, your pitcher, broken lie? / When I, your drink, go stale or dry / I am your garb, the trade you ply, / You lose your meaning, losing me."[7] Newman's famous statement that for him there had always been only two distinct vital realities, God and himself, echoes Rilke's concern.

It is a perspective which establishes both men in the modern tradition. The experience of God that each describes is primarily subjective and is in sharp contrast to the objective pattern of meaning which characterized earlier religious perception. The statements clearly suggest the interdependent nature of the relationship between God and man.

It is difficult for us as contemporary religious persons to think of God in terms other than these, that is, to envision God outside His relationship to me. So it is with reality as a whole. Its meaning is in large measure dependent on its relevance to my own situation. For better or for worse, this insight surely complicates the question of my relationship to the Father and the means by which I am to hallow His name.

But perhaps a clue to the solution lies in the very conjunction of the words "Father" and "hallow." John Dunne once pointed to the fact that Sartre's father died shortly after his son's birth and suggested that Sartre's "fatherlessness" contributed to his desire to invent or create himself, contributed then to his desire to be his own father. This image of a pure creation is perhaps the supreme illusion of life. We are born of the quickened blood and fragile hopes and despairs of our parents and we are thus marked by the ambiguity of their lives. Often we seek escape from the limitations that such a birth implies and, like Sartre, desire to create ourselves, to become the measure and foundation of things.

We seek in this way an integrity in life which seems threatened by the uneven concerns and aspirations of our parents. But to do so is to deny ourselves and our past, and to deny as well that hidden wholeness of life which we sometimes glimpse in a furtive glance of our father's eyes. The terms father and hallow are linked in an acceptance of our past that allows both self-acceptance and continuity. It allows finally an engagement with life.

Perhaps then to hallow the Father's name is to accept the gift of life, to accept the fatherhood of God. To blaspheme God is not principally to take His name in vain but to claim that we create ourselves out of nothing and that subordination or service is a kind of suicide. To blaspheme is to live in a world in which we seek a self-definition in distinguishing ourselves from others, from God. To discover one's identity is, for contemporary man, to discover alienation. We have ceased to believe in life as possessing intrinsic meaning.

The modern artist creates his meaning out of the turmoil of his own soul and in this painful and personally destructive process discovers meaning. He alone creates the meaning of his work. The work itself, marked by its singularity, does not participate in any larger pattern of meaning. Insofar as it is unique, distinctive, it has value. We have by this isolated artistic work moved from the world of the sacred to that of the profane. The two worlds remain profoundly distinct and separate realities.

But does this really correspond to our experience of meaning, of identity? In hallowing the Father's name, we return to a sense that the primary experience of our lives is relatedness to God, in whom we shall learn to relate in all our singularities to His other children. This perspective underlines our need for interdependence and a certain vital tension in man's relationship to God. Our interdependence can at times only be glimpsed metaphorically, in comparing it to the love of other fathers. In all of this we can, with Hopkins, say, "So then, my brethren, live," live joyfully and hallow the name of the Father.

For Personal Reflection

1. When have you experienced radical dependence on God and with it a desire for humble deference and submission?
2. Can you relate to the image of hallowing God's name with service? If this image is difficult, can you trace back your negative feelings and dialogue with them?

Hallowed Be Thy Name

RONDA CHERVIN

Why such a prayer? Why such a command? If God be holy within His own Trinitarian nature, why does He need us to hallow Him?

Glimpses of the mystery of God's neediness come to us in reflecting on human fatherhood. A son finds his father delightful, surprising, glorious in his hugeness—a playful giant. Though rambunctious, he accepts due punishment. He bears his father's last name proudly and speaks his first name with shy awe. I see that my husband needs that childlike adoration to fill the cup of his fatherhood to overflowing. Gabriel Marcel once wrote that whereas the mother becomes mother right away, carrying the baby in her womb, the father only gradually becomes father as he responds to the need of the child for loving protection. The first words of our daughters were "Da Da." I watched my husband, who came to fatherhood later than most, bask in his new role. As he bent down to scoop up his children, his face became more and more fatherly—kind, patient and sweet, but firm. Can it be that God, Holy in Himself, yet needs His creatures' reverent praise to become our Father, our God, our Lord?

The Jewish Sabbath, with all its encrusted deformations so criticized by Jesus, yet retained the sense of the holy and the subordination of all worldly aims to the praise of God. Through the long years of the desert, the exile, and then the Diaspora, faithful Jews have learned to abandon idols for the one true Lord.

Last summer we visited Jerusalem. I was amazed at the sense of Sabbath. The minute the sun goes down by official calculation, all but the Arab stores close. An authoritarian character in full Hasidic dress badgers passersby at the Wailing Wall Square, insisting that nothing contrary to the Sabbath rules, from knitting to holding hands, can continue. Yet a beautiful feeling of festival pervades the route to the synagogues and holy places as streams of Jews pour through the streets on foot so as not to break the Sabbath rule against driving, everyone dressed in their best, some dancing, many singing. I felt sad about our lack of Christian Sabbath in America, especially in Los Angeles, where stores are open twenty-four hours and Sunday has become the best time to go to the laundromat. Few dress up for church. Instead of being the high point around which the day is organized, most families get church over with so they can split up to pursue more important engagements.

Yet I have often experienced a spirit of holiness: sometimes during Passion Week, at liturgies celebrated by groups who know one another, where the kiss of peace becomes an expression of ongoing fellowship; or at daily mass, receiving strength in the midst of discouragement. Some charismatic groups arrange a large Sabbath dinner on Saturday evening with special prayers, singing together, reading aloud, and much wine to lighten the hearts of men and women. At one such meal I felt an ecstasy of joy, as the singing of the hymns continued far beyond the limits of some formal ceremonies.

Most often I experience the holiness of God all of a sudden in the midst of daily rounds. I might be taking out the garbage, and I'll notice a flower from the corner of my eye. Enchanted, I stand in the twilight and God's holy presence enraptures me. "Praise you, Lord," I exclaim, and mean it. The same happens often in gazing at the faces of my husband and children.

Recently God has led to what is called the "prayer of quiet" — a sense of God's presence descending to fill the soul not so much with joy as with peace. It feels very hallowed and blessed indeed.

The opposite of hallowing is mocking, vilification. Children make fun of the names of those they fear or hate. Atheists make fun of concepts of God they cannot understand. As a younster I was taught to ridicule religion. We used to enjoy going out in jeans on Easter Sunday to show that we were not involved in the national ritual of flowery bonnets and hypocritical churchgoing. I notice that as people move away from their religious practices, they enjoy making fun of the forms of their childhood piety, as if to exorcise its hold on them.

Bitter, sarcastic adolescents serve as a useful model of the rejection of hallowing. The once adored father is treated as a sham. He pushes his children into a dangerous outside world, demanding that they be courageous. He pretends to ignore their pain. He lays down unrealistic rules for them against conformity to peers, with no viable alternate plan for survival. Caught in the knowledge that they cannot bring Daddy along, cannot obey without becoming pariahs, they turn their anger against their former idol, lashing out verbally or removing themselves from the scene, faces hard with resentment.

Giving up the battle to be good and strong, the teenagers run to their companions to set up their own ideals and standards, to redeem themselves, to decide on their own nicknames or group names. Henceforth young Brown or Evans will be first and foremost a Wolf, or a Phi Sigma Chi sorority sister, or whatever.

So, too, many leave the house of the Lord because God turned out not to be a Santa Claus giving goodies and taking away sufferings. It seems that God, like Dad, will not protect us from pain, but instead makes impossible demands, insisting on moral laws that prevent us from belonging to the world into which we were tossed against our will.

And so we mock God and religion. We turn His name into a curse. We exult in our freedom from the yoke of the Church, which we caricature endlessly. Instead of celebrating holy days, we sleep late or even use our holidays to enjoy the freedom to sin.

There are many names of God: Yahweh, a symbol, not a name; I Am Who Am, manifesting God as personal and one; the Lord, Adonai. There are philosophical names: the Absolute, Pure Being, Unlimited Existence, the Supreme One. Jesus chose to reveal to us a new name—Father. He begs us to hallow *that* name. In deed after deed He tries to heal us of wrong, distrustful images of God. Jesus shows us that God does judge, but not harshly. God does punish, but not unjustly. God heals, forgives, redeems, woos. God loves as a Prodigal Father, ever ready to take the sinner back when his self-redemptive plans fail him.

Whether the idol we hallowed be money, lust, power, security, or whatever, Jesus assures us that in an instant we can be liberated from our false freedom into the childlike joy of the lilies of the fields, glorifying the Father. The Indian poet Tagore wrote, "God shatters your idol in the dust that you might know that his dust is better than your idol."

My own experience mirrors this journey from idol worship of the world to finding His house, learning to kneel, to reverence, to praise, to give glory. In times of crisis I have been tempted to flee from a God who made life so hard. Then, finding my new idols shattered, I met the Father waiting with open arms, delighted to have me back, a me who knows now that evil is futile, and my Father's gifts good.

Oh, my Father
Hallowed by Thy name
Teach me the words of life
And I shall give Thee praise
And the Father will dance

For Personal Reflection

1. Does praise and hallowing seem to you to be something important for God; for you? Describe some experiences of praise.
2. What does Sabbath mean in your life? Is this different from its meaning for your parents or yourself as a child? If you are a parent, are there ways you could make Sabbath more meaningful for your children?
3. When do you experience God's holiness most profoundly?

4. Have you ever mocked or cursed God or religion? Why? When have you been most disappointed in God or resentful of His law?
5. Have you ever put an idol before God? What? Did it fail you? Could you find your way back to God, or is that journey home still incomplete?

Chapter *3*

Meditations on Thy Kingdom Come, Thy Will Be Done, on Earth As It Is in Heaven

Thy Kingdom Come, Thy Will Be Done, on Earth As It Is in Heaven

MARY NEILL

✝ As our desire for holiness grows from meditating on our hollowness, which longs to be filled with the holiness of the Lord and His name, we naturally move, it would seem, to the second petition, "Thy will be done." Each petition of the Our Father can be seen as a lesson in the journey our consciousness must make until we are free children of the Father.

Jesus teaches us to pray *"Thy* kingdom come." We pray for freedom to do His will. Have you ever gotten bored and tired and angry with doing others' wills—your friends' and families'—and then set out to do your own, only to veer into further boredom and irritation? "The only thing worse than not getting what you want is getting what you want and finding that's not it at all," I have often muttered.

Jesus' remedy for us: to fix ourselves on what God, who created man and woman, wants us to experience.

What would God's kingdom be like here on earth? First it would mean deliverance from isolation. "It is not good for man to be alone" is the first observation made by God Himself about man, Kierkegaard notes in his *Works of Love*.

Yet how much isolation we each experience in our world, which is not yet embued with God's values, His vision! "All alone in a world I never made," one poet laments, and so do we when, as we grow more conscious, we experience more isolation and more pain of separation. When we are most deeply our authentic selves we are most singular, peculiar, "weird" — unlike anyone else. It takes real courage to love a genuine opposite; we fail to reach out to "peculiar" others, and thus our isolation grows.

Jesus meant freedom to those who followed Him because the kingdom He preached valued not your social self, your acceptable behaviors, but your hidden self. "I will not leave you orphans — I will send an advocate (a lawyer) to protect you from being alone in trials," He promises. Perhaps the tenderest act of Jesus was to express His own sense of abandonment by the Father so that all who feel orphaned by God Himself might find in Jesus a bridge over that lake of despair.

Christian communities, which hopefully guard the seed of the kingdom, do *not* deliver their members from suffering; in fact they may cause suffering. But they do offer a faith vision that assures that the meaning of our suffering is not to be found alone.

Jesus died by, through, and for others, and so can we as we help the kingdom come by refusing to withdraw into our own pain and sinfulness and neediness. God is Trinity, not an isolate; He is creator, pouring His life and energy out. So when we pray, "Thy kingdom come," we pray for grace and strength to break down our walls of isolation.

Secondly, God's kingdom means delivery from always having to prove yourself by prestige or wealth. Think of the last time you felt yourself a failure. Chances are it came from comparing yourself to some socially acceptable ideal of success or good behavior. In God's kingdom the eleventh-hour workers, the publicans and prostitutes, the marginal, the ne'er-do-wells, the lame, and the beggars from the highways and byways are all invited to the feast, to the banquet, to the marriage with God.

How far we are from fostering God's kingdom when we prize people for their prestige, success, security. How often we avoid associating with marginal types, fearing we might contaminate ourselves, that our image will falter if we do other than serve these "low-life" types. Jesus didn't just *serve* them; He ate with them, He called them friends. In God's kingdom, "high-life" and "low-life" don't matter, except perhaps for the advantage that those crying from the depths are closer to the kingdom than those burdened with success.

My father died before I finished this book, and in meditating on his gift to me and my conflicted feelings about his life and death, I came to see that in part my evaluation of him was very worldly. He was not a worldly success. He struggled on the far edges of financial stability; he had not much prestige or power.

Growing up aware of his inadequacies, I had harbored resentment that his financial and subsequent emotional insecurities had become mine. So I made sure that I have achieved financial security and prestige and success, even if in a small Bay Area puddle.

In the light of the kingdom Jesus preached, I am ashamed that I have so little honored my father's true greatness. He was extravagant in giving, prayerful, and grateful to God, never condemning his suffering. No wonder Jesus warns us that we shall be surprised at who enters the kingdom and who does not.

The eulogy I gave at Dad's funeral describes more clearly his contribution to building God's kingdom, and I share it as witness and as reparation for having so often served mammon in subtle and culturally acceptable ways:

> Today, lovingly and sorrowfully we return our earthly friend and father, Ed Neill, to our Heavenly Father who, since He has made us capable of tenderness and compassion, can be no less compassionate than we are. We are grateful for the gift of life that Dad was to us all. We are grateful that

though his life had been a hard one — that of the "poor, hard-working people, the salt of the earth" — his death was easy. He went "gentle into that Good Night"; he did not rage against the dying of the light. (Mom watched him say his prayers before he fell asleep.)

He sometimes raged against other things — loss of movement, sight, hearing — but he never raged against God. How often did we hear him say, "God has been good to me and the family. I am so grateful"? I have knelt beside him in this church, feeling his body pray beside mine, and known that for him God was not just a name, but a presence.

Dad's inner legacy to us is a rich one, which we do well to remember today. For like the earth, he was humble and gave life; like the air, he kept himself moving and alive to the end; like the fire, he was warm and generous; like the water, he could be tender and yielding. Maybe you have a favorite story of how these elements played in his life. Mine is the story of Hank, the hitchhiker he picked up near Tahoe, gave a job to, and eventually helped build a house. Early on, Hank sent for his mother, Tillie, and then Tillie sent for her parrot. I remember Mom saying firmly: "Hank's okay, Dad: Tillie has had a hard life and I can tolerate her upstairs, but the parrot — the parrot has to go." We need not pretend that Dad — and Mom, too — did not suffer at times from this openhandedness, but in an age when pride, ingratitude, stinginess, and coldness can easily be common coinage, we have in him an example of extravagance we do well not to forget. Today Dad's body returns to the earth, air, fire, and water from which it came. We carry his inner earth, air, fire, and water with us.

The third characteristic of the kingdom God would have us build on earth is one that there we would be free to function from powerlessness.

At some point we need to accept that the kingdom of God doesn't come because we prefer being admired, looking good, and being secure.

The kingdom of man seems increasingly a scramble for power and authority, with contempt for those who have no clout. Have you ever waited in a doctor's office, or any bureaucratic situation, and felt your powerlessness before impervious secretaries or nurses? The more power a person has the more distance he or she makes from you with forms, "go-betweens," and office furniture. How the poor who wait in welfare offices are made to feel their contempt- ibility! They wait and wait and wait and give further prestige to that successful man who waits for nothing—not for a taxi, not for another person, not for God.

God's kingdom is compared by Jesus to a pearl, which slowly builds itself through tiniest increments, and to a mustard seed, and to a hidden treasure, which no one finds quickly because of its hiddenness. The gifts that come in God's kingdom come through receptivity and humility. Powerlessness is not our enemy, but our friend in God's kingdom.

I feel inadequate writing of God's kingdom, though I have through my vows of poverty, chastity, and obedience sought to witness to a kingdom not based on money, family solidarity, and power over others. There are a thousand subtle ways that I undo these prom- ises and prevent God's will being done here on earth. But Jesus teaches us to pray always because He knows we will fail, the stakes are high, and the enemy strong.

When we acknowledge our weakness and our complicity in build- ing Satan's kingdom, then we can become free to accept God's power in building His kingdom. His strength, not ours, does the work. "My grace is sufficient for you, for my power is made perfect in weakness." (2 Cor. 12:9).

For Personal Reflection

1. List your memories of trying very hard to do another's will. Is it easy for you to be compliant to another? When have you been angered at your compliance?
2. When have you ever experienced boredom and irritation at having your own way? If you've never had your own way, why not?
3. List the occasions in your life when you have felt most isolated. What is your pattern of reaching to break out of isolation? Does

the "bridging" come from your vision of the kingdom or from elsewhere?

4. When have you felt "dismissed" by someone, or a group, because you were poor and (or) a failure? When have you done this to someone?

5. When have you felt most powerless? Have you ever come to see your weakness as gift?

6. In what ways do you work against the coming of God's kingdom by honoring tribal (family) solidarities, money, prestige, power?

7. If you have a different idea of what the kingdom you are praying for is, write that notion down.

Thy Kingdom Come, Thy Will Be Done, on Earth As It Is in Heaven

DON BRIEL

We pray these lines regularly, but in all likelihood we do so in the spirit of St. Augustine's prayer: "Lord, make me chaste, but not yet." Insofar as the coming of the kingdom might mark the opening to a pastoral world in which our cares would cease, our mourning transforms itself into joy, we note its appeal, but in fact we reassure ourselves that such a vision can be produced only in some distant post-apocalypse world.

For a variety of reasons, few of us truly hunger for the coming of the kingdom. The world in which we live may well seem a vale of tears, but the tears themselves are known and the litany of sin and suffering is reassuringly familiar. In our commonplace world there is nothing new under the sun, and we are, for the most part, content to have it so.

Most people believe, according to Kierkegaard, that the command to love one's neighbor as oneself is "intentionally a little too severe — like putting the clock ahead half an hour to make people sure of not being late in the morning." Similarly, we pray for the kingdom, for the transformation of the world in the image of heaven,

52

but we tend to mean by this hyperbolic imagery merely a gradual process of self-improvement. We would like to be kinder and more generous.

In liturgies, our prayers of petition emphasize the search for abstract values or immediate consolation in moments of crisis. They are rarely marked by prophetic insight. We have domesticated the kingdom, filling it with pots and pans and easychairs, the familiar furnishings of our souls. We tend to view the kingdom as the fulfillment of our present condition rather than a radically new reality which might demand our conversion.

Nonetheless, we do know that in some sense the kingdom is associated not only with peace but with the sword. Whether the violent who bear it away do so in the name of the kingdom or in opposition to it is a matter of debate among Scripture scholars, but it is surely true that the acceptance of the kingdom can be seen to be the occasion of a violent uprooting of one's customary condition.

If there is a certain violence associated with the coming of the kingdom, how can we understand Christ's caution that the kingdom of heaven is reserved for the childlike? That the kingdom is reserved for those who become like children strikes us as somewhat paradoxical, for in our own time we have come to accept Dickens's vision of the child as innocent victim of a manipulative and violent world. Childhood should be, we think, a period of peace and tranquility that precedes the turbulence of adolescence, the transition stage to adulthood.

We often hear complaints that children are maturing too quickly today, that the period of innocence is increasingly shortened. Drugs are sold and used in school yards; children are beginning sexual relationships at an earlier age; five-year-olds are told in television commercials that they can vicariously celebrate the joys of high school life with a doll who is a popular cheerleader, blond and curvaceous, the object of desire of all boy dolls.

All of this seems to point to an ambivalent attitude toward children in contemporary society. We proclaim the value of childhood innocence; we celebrate it in our Christmas cards and charity appeals, but at the same time, we recognize that this innocence is really only naiveté, in itself unreal, valuable only because to confront the real world too early is to be overwhelmed.

And so we encourage our children to believe in Santa Claus for one more year and not to spoil it for the younger children, not because this allows the child to live in the world of reality, but because the false security of the illusion has the greater appeal.

From this point of view, although we may yearn for its peace and contentment, childhood is that which is necessarily left behind as we confront the "real world." At best we might hope that our adult perspective will be marked by a certain simplicity and humility, the virtues of the child.

This suggests a profoundly cynical view of the possibilities and purposes of the human condition; but, more than that, an essentially romantic vision of the nature of childhood prohibits any real understanding of the relationship of the child to the kingdom.

It is perhaps not the native innocence of children that qualifies them for the kingdom. As a parent, I continually marvel at the cunning of the youthful mind. Rather, what may allow the opening to the kingdom is the very violence with which children embrace their interests. They leave all behind them, if only for the moment, in the headlong pursuit of the particular object they desire, and so they are transformed in their initial possession of it.

As adults, we distance ourselves from our longings. We operate out of a fundamental detachment, fearing that we might lose ourselves in our desire for the other. We emphasize the adult virtues of temperance and prudence, and it may well be that these virtues, so perceived, are obstacles to the kingdom. They isolate us from that which we desire, and so, unlike children, we define ourselves in isolation from, rather than in relation to, that which we seek, that which we love.

We seek to ensure a kind of autonomy, but as Michael Novak writes, one of the results of the American pursuit of autonomy is "heteronomy," the condition of living under laws that are not our own. We live apart from our institutions. In order to guarantee our independence, we are no longer what Gabriel Marcel called *disponible*, or "available to others," and perhaps similarly we are not available to the kingdom.

We live in splendid isolation, and in an age in which the need for interdependence has never been more evident, we devote our efforts to acquiring do-it-yourself skills.

As Americans we have not recovered from the shock of the 1973-74 oil embargo, when a handful of Arabs forced us to alter our lifestyles and our expectations. This was further aggravated by the humiliation of the hostage crisis in Iran. With some truth, State Department spokesmen emphasized that we had won this particular struggle because the Iranians had been discredited in the international community. But if this was winning, many wondered what it might mean to lose.

We had always thought that winning in a situation meant imposing our will on others or at least avoiding the necessity of any compromise. To win was to maintain our autonomy in the world, while lesser nations, such as Britain, were forced to accept new realities produced by events outside their control.

There is a cruel irony in this alienation which is the result of our search for autonomy. We need to open ourselves to the lessons of childhood. We are required to abandon the illusion of autonomy and accept the obligation of mutual interdependence. To do so is to open ourselves to conversion. It is only the child who can be converted by the truth, because he recognizes that he and the truth are not exactly the same thing. To become childlike is not to return to the state of innocence but to escape a world of self-satisfaction and to become available to others and the truth.

And so it is as adults that we look with some ambivalence to the coming of the kingdom, but perhaps there are other reservations as well. Like Dostoevski's Grand Inquisitor, we hesitate to accept the full mystery of the Christian message. Like him, we too might be willing to sacrifice Christ rather than open ourselves to the reality of the kingdom. We know that the Christian message is at best bittersweet, that here death and life are curiously interrelated, and that suffering and salvation are not mutually exclusive. There is much that is unsettling to the adult who looks forward to the coming of the kingdom. It is true that we see the traces of God everywhere, but they are not always reassuring. From many points of view there is little reason to presume God's love and perhaps even less to welcome it. Robert Griffin reminds us that Scripture confirms that God has an interest in the falling sparrow, but so too has the professional ornithologist. What distinguishes their concern? Must we always seek the traces of God in the ravaged faces of mankind, faces marked by hunger, by fear, by hatred, by cancer, by despair? Is there no alternative to this love that chastens and refines? We are surrounded by images of suffering that seem to demean any value in life.

We do know that in earlier, pre-morphia times the grim and painful reality of death was commonly encountered in public halls for the dying that were hung with monumental representations of the crucifixion as the primary image of hope. Today such suffering strikes us as both unnecessary and slightly barbarous.

We seek what Father Griffin calls the wind currents to the sun, but we have little reason to suspect that the kingdom of God is marked by a tropical climate. St. Matthew has told us that Jesus said, "It is not those who say to me 'Lord, Lord' who will enter the kingdom of heaven, but the person who does the will of my Father in heaven." We know then that to do the will of the Father is to open ourselves to the kingdom (and too, that to do the will of the Father has something to do with becoming childlike), but again, to embrace the Father's will is to confront the reality of death. The love of such a father gives us pause.

One of Flannery O'Connor's characters in *The Violent Bear It Away*, speaking of the problem of the will of God, was led to ask, "Who is this blue-cold child and this woman, plain as the winter? Is this the Word of God, this blue-cold child? Is this His will, this plain winter woman? . . . Love cuts like the cold wind and the will of God is plain as the winter. Where is the summer will of God? Where are the green seasons of God's will? Where is the spring and summer of God's will?" These are the questions we ask. These are the adult questions.

We are aware that to pray for the coming of the kingdom, to

pray that God's will be done, is to open our lives to the acceptance of a series of paradoxes. Thoreau once said that most people live lives of quiet desperation. As we cling to the familiar, the secure, our lives risk becoming increasingly grotesque and deformed.

We persist in the illusion of automony and close ourselves to grace. We live out shrunken and desperate stories. Only the child has the courage — we tend to say the naiveté — to embrace the truth violently and to risk living out the apparent contradictions. It is in this sense that the life of a child is graced. To be a child is to admit one's dependence, to accept the Father, and to open oneself to the kingdom.

For Personal Reflection

1. In what sense have you experienced suffering to be related to the violence which opens to the kingdom?
2. What sufferings most lead you to distrust God's providence? How have you reconciled yourself to that distrust?
3. In what ways do you feel called to be more childlike in the intensity of your living?
4. Is it easy or hard for you to conceive of yourself as being violent for the kingdom? In what sense do you think that a comfortable life might be an obstacle to the kingdom?

Thy Kingdom Come, Thy Will Be Done, on Earth As It Is in Heaven

RONDA CHERVIN

As I pray the next two lines of the Our Father, "Thy kingdom come, Thy will be done, on earth as it is in heaven," I am impressed with their austerity. "Our Father" is warm and communal, "hallowed" is bright and ecstatic, but now we come to the hard part. Am I sensing the fierceness of Jesus' longing for the Father's kingdom to come, on earth as it is in heaven?

Rereading the Gospel of Matthew slowly while working on a Scripture project, I was impressed by how much a prophet Jesus was in fighting for God's rights in a distorted world. I feel his passionate concern for the disparity between the Father's will and the people's folly. Seeking happiness in the wrong places, they destroy themselves while breaking the Father's heart.

As a teacher of Catholic ethics to an unwilling generation, I myself experience prophetic anguish. How can I awaken my students from their drugged sleep that they might become soldiers for the kingdom? How? Jesus tells me how in the prayer he taught us. Never separate the kingdom from the Father. Never make it seem that sacrifice is an end in itself without reference to the building of the Father's kingdom of joy and love.

What, then, is the kingdom of heaven Jesus preached? Was it a utopian dream He played with in melancholy moments, imagining how it would be if only He were to become a successful Messiah instead of a crucified savior? Was it the heavenly fulfillment of the beatitudes, the world to come where the poor in spirit would be blessed, the mournful comforted, the meek would inherit the earth, the righteous be satisfied, the merciful receive mercy, the pure in heart see God, and the persecuted get their reward? (Matt. 5:1-12). Surely that is part of the promise of the kingdom, but it does not fulfill the prayer that the kingdom come *on earth* as it is in heaven.

Perhaps the kingdom of heaven on earth is the paradox of the parables—the mixed wheat and weeds, the seed hidden, the leaven buried, the rejection of the true King in the crowning with thorns. "All the way to heaven is heaven," exclaimed St. Catherine of Siena. If this is true, then the kingdom we pray to come must be both here and there, in time and in eternity (Matt. 13:36-43).

The kingdom is coming whenever we long for it, ready to sell all for the treasure. It is in the child's raging cry for justice in the sandbox. It is in the teen's longing for perfect sincerity. It is in the businessman's disgust with his own compromises. It is in the mother's seeking of ways to bring up her children to be good. It is in the elderly man's futile wish that he could relive his life with wisdom.

The kingdom is coming for me whenever I let Christ be king,

Lord of my life, when I open myself to discoveries of God's will. Of late, this has meant long hours spent in learning how to prepare healthy foods to replace the tasty junk I used to serve my family. Surprising peace comes now when I watch my husband and children at dinner. In the future, it may mean tending a sick mother or husband. For me that requires a giant leap of faith, to give up the glimpses of beatitude to be had in "doing my own thing" for the sake of the kingdom on earth built up by selfless love.

Finding Christ in the midst of daily life also has come to mean for me stripping off the husk of the deed to get to the core of the love behind it. A prey to middle-aged malaise, I often find tasks which previously delighted me now becoming tedious. St. Francis de Sales, in the treatise *On the Love of God*, teaches that it is part of the process of loving God above all things that we develop a distaste for acts previously accomplished more out of pride and concupisence than for the kingdom. As our interest palls we may succumb to inertia. This can only be combatted by a radical giving of the self to God as the only source of perfect happiness, followed by a willingness to do good for the sake of fulfilling His holy will.

Such a process may sound at first rather grim. But that is only when we view it as an intellectual truth. The joy in God that comes from surrender is what gives us grace to be happy to do each small thing that builds up the kingdom of love. When, in startling contrast to a previous stance of resented routine, those who live with us find us so eager to serve, fresh tenderness will come to the fore.

I wrote a short poem to this effect when returning to family life after a beautiful vacation cruising up the coast of Norway:

Homecoming

from glory in the whole
to piecework in my niche?
from contemplation to action?
descent from heaven?

No, lifting up the earth—
"Thy kingdom come."

So doing God's will has come to mean for me not only greater sacrifice but also much greater joy. I hear the Father asking me to join His dance by loving myself as His beloved child. I hear Him reading the Beatitudes to me and saying, "Dear one, I know your poverty of spirit and I am eager to give you overflowing joy, if only you will take your eyes off your problems and direct them to my gifts. I want to comfort you for all your tears, if only you would cease groaning long enough to come to me in prayer. Open your eyes, my beloved disciple, and see the beauty of the earth that is ours. As you fight for your prolife cause, hold fast to my justice and also my mercy, believing those you pray for will one day be saved. Stop finding reasons for self-hatred and acknowledge your own purity of heart that you might take hope in the promise of your unity with Me for all eternity in the kingdom. Draw close to me and see that it is my crucified son who wants to wash the spit of your enemies away with his own blood."

> Yes, my God, my Lord, My Father
> I exult in being a woman of the kingdom.
> Yes, my God, My Lord, My Father
> I know that your kingdom is coming.
> *Where the Father will dance*

For Personal Reflection

1. How do you respond to Jesus as prophet?
2. When have you played the role of prophet in the past, present, or possibly the future?
3. Where have you seen longing for the kingdom?
4. What impresses you as representing the kingdom already now on earth?
5. What does doing God's will mean for you now in your daily life?
6. Does God want more joy for you than you allow yourself?

Chapter **4**

Meditations on Give Us This Day Our Daily Bread

Give Us This Day Our Daily Bread

MARY NEILL

✝ A central miracle of Jesus' life, the one preceding His discon-certing promise to give His body and blood, which caused many to leave Him, was the multiplication of the fishes and the loaves. So when I come to the central petition of the Our Father for daily bread, I pause to reflect about the mystery of the multiplication of bread.

We live in a world where over and over we hear that there is not enough. There is not enough bread — over half of the world goes to bed hungry every night; there is not enough oil; we are running out of water and even fresh air, which our ancestors never dreamed was a fragile tent above our earth.

In smaller circles I hear, "There are not enough priests; there are not enough sisters; there are not enough men to go around. There is not enough . . . . There is not enough," the world chants, and so we hoard.

61

Yet there is enough to go around—enough food, enough of nature's resources, enough money, enough people, enough of everything when we live from the consciousness inculcated by the Our Father. Always the plural reigns: "our" . . . "us" . . . *our* bread.

It is only when we ask for *our* bread, not my bread, from *our* Father, not *my* Father, that there is enough to go around. When we know that we are all children of the same Heavenly Father, of the same mother earth, all will be fed, and abundantly—with "twelve baskets of fragments" remaining.

You have only to read Francis Moore Lappe's *Food First* to be convinced that the solution to the world hunger problem lies in changing the consciousness of people, not in giving handouts to small nations—handouts that only further impoverish them. How can God answer any of our private prayers for health, wealth, cure, when we ignore the cry of the hungry peoples of the world?

I wonder sometimes if there exists at all a private Father in heaven who answers private concerns. I wonder also: Are there any *private* concerns? These are hard thoughts for one instructed so often in building my private relationship to God, for surely that has been the connotation of spirituality in the West, and indeed this distortion of Western spirituality must be in part responsible for the world's present disarray. The richer a person is, the more he or she possesses things singly. A private home, a private car, a private phone, a private beach, a private yacht, a private island. Richness buys private space. Poor people have no private rooms, or even private beds.

Surely this isolated singleness from richness is what Jesus admonishes against when He warns that only with difficulty shall the rich man enter the kingdom of heaven. Alone, independent, controlling my own goods, space, money, and time—*isolated*—how can I receive life from another's hands, from the Father's hands? The anguish of the age is loneliness: "No mama, no papa, no Uncle Sam," the marines of Bataan sang. It is only when we act as brothers that we experience the Father. We are rich when we are interdependent; bankrupt, stingy, and haunted when we seek to control our space.

When the apostles ask Jesus to teach them to pray, for they see that it is His nights alone in prayer that give him strength, He teaches them to *ask*. He teaches, as it were, to be "empty, be a receiver, own your creatureliness."

The Moslems feel that the lack of acceptance of our creaturehood is the central obstacle to union with God, and so the muezzins call them to fall flat on their faces five times a day. Flat on the earth, mother from which my dust came and to which it shall return, my consciousness is far different than when I stand, walk, reach, or grab, or even when I kneel. Try it and see.

Flat on the ground, we are humbled (near the humus to which we shall return), and it is from this position, too, that we can at times perhaps best listen to those other hungers within, which need our daily attention and supplication.

When attuned to my deep ambivalence and restlessness, I touch upon the hunger to have my being fed by the confirmation of others. I need someone to see me, to respect, to say, "Yes, you count."

Certainly this was one of the kinds of heavenly bread that Jesus fed to His followers, confirming their presence, their gifts, their importance to the kingdom. Looking into Jesus' eyes, sinners, successful men, small children, prostitutes, Pharisees all saw His loving attention, which said, "You count; your being makes a difference to me and to the Father."

Have you ever had the experience of watching someone's eyes brim with tears as you listened carefully to their story? My sense is that the tears signal relief and release: "I am heard, finally."

Martin Buber considers the greatest evil we extend to others to be the witholding of the bread of confirmation. We need not necessarily agree with someone (confirmation may demand con-. frontation) but seek to affirm that each person is also, like Jesus, God's word and imagination made flesh. Everyone mirrors something of God, and if I cannot learn to see that, I will never see God. "It is from one person to another that the heavenly bread of self-being is passed," Buber reminds us.

It well may be that our inability to feed the physically hungry of the world is connected to our inability to name and feed our own hunger for confirmation. When I can, through the confirmation given and received by others, know that I count, the power is released in me to make a difference, to help others to know they count. If I don't count, how can I make a difference? How can I feed others from the bread of my being if I don't like the taste of me?

The Lord Jesus broke His life open, shared the bread of His self-being for us, and this is the example we must follow. But the courage to feed others from our own broken lives can come only if we daily beg the Father to fill our deep hunger for confirmation. How did Jesus ever know He could feed His followers from His broken body as well as from His miracles unless He opened himself through prayer to the Father's confirmation: "This is my beloved son."

Before Jesus ever began His ministry or did even one thing publically to glorify His Father, the Father expressed His pleasure in Jesus. Wonderful consolation for us who know well our deep desire to be loved for what we are, not just for what we do. Jesus was not afraid to beg for support and confirmation. "Do you love me? Do you love me? Do you love me more than these?" he begs Peter, who is rightly taken aback. Jesus was not distant from His hungers; humbly he expressed them, whether for water, bread, comfort, or love. And neither must we be distant from ours. For it is our hunger for him that effects our holiness, that helps us build God's kingdom: "Blessed are they that hunger and thirst . . ."

For Personal Reflection

1. Are you aware of the times when you fear that there is not enough? That you are not enough? What kinds of things are you tempted to hoard? List these and try to figure out what inner hunger they might symbolize.
2. What is your reaction to pictures and articles portraying world hunger? What actions have you considered for addressing this problem, or do you feel it is impossible for you to make any difference?

3. To what degree do you envy the power of privacy that the rich have? Do you hate to share the phone, the TV, the car? To what degree are your family quarrels centered around the common usage of material goods?
4. Record any experience you have had of being deeply confirmed by another. Have you ever had in meditation the experience of feeling that God the Father or Jesus was saying, "You are my beloved child in whom I am well pleased"?
5. Would you describe yourself as a confirming person, or is it hard for you to praise others? Is it hard to accept praise?
6. Ask someone you know to tell you why they love you. Be aware of any difficulty in asking or in receiving this information. Read John 21 and dialogue with Jesus about His hunger for love.

Give Us This Day Our Daily Bread

DON BRIEL

I remember once reading that the diet of the average peasant in mediaeval Europe consisted largely of bread with occasional vegetables and perhaps on great feasts meat or eggs. The writer hastened to add that the bread was, unlike our refined variety, relatively nutritious. Clearly, for the peasant bread was the staff of life, and I was struck at the time by the enormous distance that separates us.

We no longer live in the peasant's world, for better and for worse, and this transition implies a good deal more than merely a change in our eating habits. We are, in our own time, part of a consumer society, divorced from the goods we consume, knowing little of their origins or the nature of their effects.

We buy our bread processed and packaged and worry about carcinogens. "Sesame Street" is reduced to a detailed description of where potatoes and milk come from. We are all becoming increasingly like urban children bused to a farm in order to experience "nature." In this sense we are divided selves, separated somehow from our roots.

Still we are seized with a nostalgia for the land, and often, decked in imitation peasant garb, we spend our weekends struggling with a vegetable garden and admiring our neighbor's compost. This is not merely a part of a romantic longing for a simpler time. We seek to participate in the cosmic order and often feel that our transient progressive world has lost touch with its natural base. We seek to participate in eternal verities and gaze at our ripening tomatoes with envy as well as satisfaction. We look with some skepticism for a more harmonious understanding of life.

For mediaeval man bread was a known quantity, fruit of the earth and product of his own labor. Because he knew well both its material quality and its relationship to life, he was freed to an awareness of its symbolic capacity. The bread had not only a functional but also a real value. It demonstrated a certain unified vision of life in which nature and spirit were intermingled. In large measure this awareness accounts for the mediaeval preoccupation with explaining the nature of the relationship between the worlds of matter and spirit.

People of the period sensed the curious interdependence and intimate tension that bound the two in the person of Christ. Perhaps this too explains the fascination of the mediaeval world with the person of Mary — Mary the symbol of human participation in the divine. And thus cathedral after cathedral rose in her honor, commemorating her communion with God but also celebrating the glory of the human condition, freed by the Incarnation to a similar participation in the life of God.

The world of the Middle Ages was an unusually optimistic one, a thoroughly hierarchical society based on an absolutely democratic principle, the commonality of the human condition. Its principle of unity, then, was a real one, with a distinctively sacramental character which allowed it to exercise an integrating function. Whatever the superficial distinctions among persons, to speak of the bread of life was to refocus a pattern of meaning of which Christ was the center and the community as a whole its expression. The Eucharist was at the heart of mediaeval devotion and poetry. The great quest was the search for the Holy Grail, the encounter with the sacrament which would fully realize the partial understanding of life and meaning.

In contrast, paradoxically, ours is a democratic society based on a distinctively hierarchical principle. Because we operate out of a utilitarian standpoint, we speak of human worth in terms of our capacity to exercise influence over others, to make a mark on society. Quite simply, the principle of unity in contemporary society is power. Ironically, as a principle of unity it contains the very source of its own destruction.

Nonetheless, we tend to give weapons instead of bread to those in need, and even to ourselves. Weapons are the great equalizers, and we comfort ourselves with a slippery understanding of balance of power. The principle of unity is no longer commonality but equality, but this is a consistently shifting principle which demands a degree of vigilance and distrust if it is to be measured accurately, and so we are enslaved to a quality of envy and mutual suspicion.

Maritain once said that bread for others was a spiritual question, whereas bread for oneself was a material one. Power not only corrupts, it also alienates, and as a result, in modern society the very idea of community begins to strike us as artificial. We have come in our own time to a vital awareness of the singularity of our personalities, our temperaments, our approaches to the real, but this awareness has become a fixed principle which serves to isolate us from others and from life.

When Bultmann says so forcefully that "now it is either/or. Now the question is whether a man really wants God and his kingdom or the world and its goods, and the decision must be made radically,"[8] we smile at the simplicity of it all. Nothing is evil in itself, we remind ourselves; all things are capable of being used to a good end.

But Scriptural warnings about wealth all seem to caution centrally against making oneself the measure of things. Wealth is an obstacle to spiritual life precisely because it provides the illusion of control, of power. I recently read an article in the *Catholic Worker* which spoke of the spiritual quality of waiting—in patience, in humility—a gift in large measure reserved for the poor, and like all gifts not without its share of pain.

We hate to be kept waiting, hate the feelings of dependence and powerlessness it raises in us. We have better things to do than wait, but again, it is in waiting that we attune ourselves to the presence and the demands of others.

Josef Pieper has said that leisure is the basis of culture largely because it opens us to a communal consciousness and at the same time an awareness of our own uniqueness: In contrast, we say that leisure is a luxury few can afford in such unpropitious times. Leisure is for those on welfare or perhaps for government employees who refuse the larger challenges of life. But in many ways, we have forgotten the meaning of the word.

It is commonplace to apologize to others for the fact that we have not been more productive in our free time. We confuse leisure with boredom, but as Kierkegaard reminds us, "Idleness is not an evil, indeed one may say that every human being who lacks a sense for idleness proves that his consciousness has not yet been elevated to the level of the humane."[9]

Idleness opens our lives to intrusions, to criticism, and thus to the possibility of conversion. In this sense, to be human is to accept a basic tension between our singularity and our dependence on others and on God. As a result the unity or personal integrity of a man made whole is produced by a tension between those two qualities of uniqueness and dependence—a poise which is achieved not by a simple resolution in favor of the preferred pole, but in a process of delicate discrimination between them.

This is what Bonhoeffer implies when he says that "in the center between me and myself, the old and the new existence. . . . Here Christ stands."[10] We remain in need of a mediator to integrate the polarity of our lives, of our consciousness. Insofar as we live only in our singularity, we choose to live in alienation. This is the very appeal of wealth and, in one sense, its own reward.

There has been an interesting change in our attitude toward wealth in recent history. In the past greed was always considered unromantic and unspectacular and was classified among the cold-hearted, less appealing sins. One has only to think of Scrooge for example.

In our own time, however, "covetousness has been endowed with a glamour on a big scale." How can we explain the interest evoked by the life and death of such a pathetic figure as Howard Hughes or the extraordinary popularity of television programs such as "Dallas"? These are shrunken, grotesque lives. What is the attraction and what does it indicate? Surely it is largely the power, the control that we associate with great wealth which intrigues us. Although there is a basically dehumanizing distortion here, greed has been given the status of a respectable sin.

Writing in the 1940s, Dorothy Sayers asked, "Do, for instance, the officials stationed at the church doors in Italy to exclude women with bare arms or legs ever turn anyone away on the grounds that he is too well dressed to be honest?" And again, "When we go to a movie and see a film about empty-headed people in luxurious surroundings, do we say 'What drivel!'or do we sit in a misty dream, wishing we could give up our daily work and marry into surroundings like that?"[11]

We need to restore balance in our illusory evaluations of others. How often do we fight the tendency to assess the quality of a person's life, or a possession, or a work of art by its dollar value? What other measurement is possible? Why do we collect stamps, art, or acquire a house — because they enhance our appreciation of life or because they provide a hedge against inflation?

Again Dorothy Sayers warns us about the fact that "it is becoming very evident that until this emphasis is readjusted the economic balance sheet will have to be written in blood."

Insofar as we seek an integration of our lives, we must somehow open ourselves more fully to dependence and at the same time to discovering a deeper sense of our own singularity. This involves an acceptance of the complexity of a relationship with God which unceasingly calls us to conversion, to what Von Hügel calls a "costly but noble state of tension" in which the fullness of humanity might be realized.

For Personal Reflection

1. Have you experienced any changes in the kinds of food you consume and the ways you prepare and garden it in recent years? Has this been related to spiritual growth, and in what ways?
2. In which areas of your life do you maintain individual control and in which do you seek community interdependence? Do you see any need for change?
3. When have you felt a radical call to choose between God's kingdom and the world and its goods?
4. What are your attitudes toward leisure? How often have you apologized because you have not been more productive?
5. How do you react to waiting? To any situations where you lack control?
6. How does assessment of others in terms of measurable succcess limit your ability to love others and self?

Give Us This Day Our Daily Bread

RONDA CHERVIN

I feel ashamed to start this chapter, I who have never known a day's hunger. Jesus did not feel ashamed. He identified Himself with the poor and knew their basic need for the staff of life. Let me here acknowledge my gratitude that my Father set me down in a land of plenty in a family of hard workers concerned for my welfare, and that I have never lacked a job, a good salary. I am happy to feel obligated to give to the really poor as Christ teaches.

Yet I have other most urgent hungers. The daily bread can be whatever is absolutely necessary for survival, be that bread, love, grace, Eucharist. Being one brought up to take bread for granted, it was always for love I craved. Given abundant love from my mother, I never got used to the idea that the world outside might not love me. I have learned painfully indeed that love is God's gift, not my birthright. And I have often found that when love from humans is in short supply, God can comfort me if I would ask. Some say, "How? How can God supply the immediate love we desire so much?" I can only reply that I have experienced it. In despair I lie flat on the floor and have a hunger strike. "God," I call, "if You want me to go on, give me Your love!" And He has not failed to hear my cry.

Before my conversion I went to daily Mass, drawn by its mysteries. Without any special sense of Christ's presence, I felt a great need for the Eucharist, which gradually became a hunger. A priest I knew once spoke derisively of daily communicants as addicts. I like to think that Jesus is happy if we come to draw our strength first each day from Him. It is documented that some saints ate nothing but this holy bread. I believe it.

Last summer, touring the city of London, I had a striking communal experience of addiction to Jesus in the Eucharist. Traveling, I had resigned myself to missing my "daily bread," the Eucharist, but still hoped that somehow God would lead my steps to a Catholic church just at the right moment for the Mass.

The first day, after struggles with the airport, luggage, lost hotels, etc., I found myself near the Roman Catholic cathedral at 5:00 P.M. Might there be an evening Mass? I read the schedule eagerly. Sure enough—5:30 P.M. Great delight. Added joy, I had come in upon a rehearsal of one of my favorite musical works, Elgar's *The Dream of Gerontius*, based on Cardinal Newman's poem.

But it turned out that for the first time in many years they were canceling the 5:30 Mass because of the conflict with the rehearsal. When I asked a passing priest if I might receive communion being a tourist, he looked at me in horror. Didn't I know the rubrics? No liturgy, no communion. This rule is broken in some countries for tourists, but not, evidently, in proper England.

I went back to my pew disconsolate and began to wonder how the usual evening Mass people were taking it. They had the marvelous choir singing snatches of celestial music, true, but I knew they would be hungry for the heavenly dinner they had expected, for they were, like me, big-city "church mice": poor, desperate, for whom the Eucharist is the great joy of the day.

At little after the scheduled time, however, I began to notice a trickle of people heading for the rear of the church and down a staircase. I followed. Sure enough, downstairs in the crypt a priest of the people had understood their need. Jammed in a circle we watched this young Franciscan say the Mass slowly, oh so slowly, his eyes glued to the Host as if he were seeing the Lord right before him. From above we heard the yearning strains of Gerontius on his way to heaven, and I thought of how Cardinal Newman had loved the Eucharist so urgently and music next. Was it not he who said that music was not of the earth but something that had escaped from heaven! Was it he who knew that the little ones of Christ, me included, would never be satisfied with beauty instead of God-bread?

Jesus, earthy as well as ethereal, taught us to pray for our daily bread, but not for luxuries. The issue of what is luxury and what is necessity has long plagued middle-class Christians eager to obey the commandment to give generously but unsure how much. Of late I have heard the distinction made quite insightfully between what we need and what we want. What we need is both what is basic to human decency and also what an individual must have to develop his or her talents. So for one a cello would be a necessity, for another a pretentious showpiece. For one a car is a necessity to get to work, for another an ego trip.

The joy of poor saints like Francis of Assisi or Mother Teresa of Calcutta gives us pause. Are our luxuries friends or perhaps enemies of real happiness? It makes me heavy of body to overeat, heavy of spirit to spend hours servicing gadgets. It makes me feel deliciously light to share good food, lighter still to give away piles of clothing, books, money.

Saul Bellow, in his novels, likes to portray heroes with gargantuan appetites for the good things of life and even more for nameless metaphysical fulfillment that never comes. In one book his main character is afflicted with afternoon pangs of desire. In agony he cries out every day, "I want, I want, I want!" unsure even of the object of his great need. At the end of the book, chastened by a stay with a tight community of African villagers, he comes back saying, "They want, they want, they want," sure that the meaning of life is not to fulfill oneself but others. As Christians anxious to build the kingdom we must have the greatest concern about prayers of the really poor for daily bread. We must initiate or support social justice programs.

Seeking first the kingdom seems to me to be related to the order of the petitions in the Our Father. We do not begin by laying out our need for daily bread. First we acknowledge the Father, then we praise His name, then we commit ourselves to bringing about the kingdom of heaven. Having renewed our loyalty to our Father in this way, we are then permitted to ask for our own needs. All my life I am sure I will struggle with the mystery of the truth that God is the center yet He creates us with a natural self-centeredness. The drama of our salvation seems always to consist in God's drawing us out of ourselves into essential relation to Him, to our brothers and sisters, to the world around us, then showing us how expanded we have become in the process. But each time our self-transcendence leads to pain, we recoil back into ourselves like snails, pretending that we alone truly exist.

The Gospels constantly challenge the most basic assumptions of our self-centered mentality. Again and again Jesus tells us that we need not worry about food and clothing. What counts is working for the kingdom of heaven, for that is where we will dwell if only we fit ourselves for it by weaving a garment of love. As novices of that kingdom we are not allowed to put survival in the worldly kingdom first. What lack of faith is revealed when Christians excuse themselves for immoral acts with the words "I had to do it. After all, you gotta survive."

Even without focusing on the rewards of eternal life, it can be seen that making survival the prime goal is contrary to human dignity. An autobiographical narrative of Sister Maria Jose Hobday, a Native American sister, illustrates this point:

> We were rather poor during the 1930s; not desperately so, but poor enough to feel the lacks and to live on the edge of insecurity. One Saturday evening I was working late on my homework. I was in the living room, my brothers were out-

side with their friends, and my parents were in the kitchen, discussing our financial situation. It was very quiet, and I found myself more and more following the kitchen conversation, rather than attending to my homework. Mama and Daddy were talking about what had to be paid for during the week, and there was very little money—a few dollars. As I listened, I became more and more anxious, realizing that there was not enough to go around. They spoke of school needs, of fuel bills, of food. Suddenly, the conversation stopped, and my mother came into the room where I was studying. She put the money—a couple of bills and a handful of change—on the desk. "Here," she said, "go find two or three of your brothers and run to the drugstore before it closes. Use this money to buy strawberry ice cream."

I was astonished! I was a smart little girl, and I knew we needed this money for essentials. So I objected. "What? We have to use this to pay bills, Mama, to buy school things. We can't spend this for ice cream!" Then I added, "I'm going to ask Daddy." So I went to my father, telling him what Mother had asked me to do. Daddy looked at me a moment, then threw back his head and laughed. "Your mother is right, honey," he said. "When we get this worried about a few dollars, we are better off having nothing at all. We can't solve all the problems, so maybe we should celebrate instead. Do as your mother says."

So I collected my brothers and we went to the drugstore. In those days you could get a lot of ice cream for a few dollars, and we came home with our arms full of packages. My mother had set the table, made fresh coffee, put out what cookies we had, and invited in the neighbors. It was a great party! I do not remember what happened concerning the other needs, but I remember the freedom and fun of that evening. I thought about that evening many times, and came to realize that spending a little money at that time for pleasure was not irresponsible. It was a matter of survival of the spirit. The bills must have been paid; we made it through the weeks and months that followed. I learned that my parents were not going to allow money to dominate them. I learned something of the value of money, of its use. I saw that of itself it was not important but that my attitude toward it affected my own spirit, could reduce me to powerlessness or give me power of soul.

A spiritual truth related to that of Sister Hobday that often comes to mind when I pray, "Give us our *daily* bread," is Jesus' wisdom in urging us to live each day without anxiety for the future. I am sure that if I made a list of every unhappy thought during a twenty-four-hour period, most of them would not be about present woe but rather about future possibilities. Being temporal creatures, there is no way that we can escape a natural feeling for past and future. We are neither animal nor God, to live solely in the now. Yet there is a Christian way to approach past, present, and future, quite different from the ordinary way. Sören Kierkegaard, the Danish philosopher-theologian, described the different forms of time characteristic of those living in a hedonistic stage, an ethical stage, and a religious stage. The hedonist, bent on pleasure seeking, culls the past for satisfying memories, tries to hold a happy present still, then plots how to manipulate the future. The ethical person views the past as cause of remorse, the present as duty, and the future as opportunity for good deeds. The religiously centered person views the past with contrition and gratitude, the present as a moment of union with God, and the future as providence and eternity. So for the hedonist the prayer for daily bread really means no more than obtaining enough pleasure to tip the balance of dissatisfactions and satisfactions. For the ethical man that bread is fuel for his projects. For the religious person it is a pure gift, sign of God's continual pouring out of life to us, His beloved children.

> O Father God
> Fill us with the bread that we need
> Now and for eternity . . . .
> *"Where the Father will dance"*

For Personal Reflection

1. Have you ever been without food?
2. What is your most urgent hunger?
3. How do you feel about receiving Jesus as the bread of the Eucharist?

4. What for you is necessity, what luxury?
5. Could you be as free as Sister Hobday's parents about celebration in the midst of want?
6. What concern do you show for social justice?
7. Do you see yourself as more like a hedonist, ethical, or religious person in relationship to ways of viewing past, present, and future?

Chapter **5**

Meditations on Forgive Us Our Trespasses As We Forgive Those Who Trespass Against Us

And Forgive Us Our Trespasses As We Forgive Those Who Trespass Against Us

MARY NEILL

† *Whatever happened to sin?*" Karl Menninger asks, and rare it is that one hears public or private sinners turn to those offended and say "I did it, and I'm sorry." Yet the acknowledgment of one's own sinfulness releases the compassion which allows us to forgive the many injuries we sustain throughout our lives.

Martin Buber thinks that the inability of modern men and women to own their sinfulness may arise from a false relationship to guilt. In his wise lecture "Guilt and Guilt Feelings," he warns that if we would take away man's capacity for guilt by labeling it mere "taboo" or only neurotic, we take away one of the greatest human powers—a power which separates and elevates man. "Man is the being who is capable of becoming guilty and is capable of illuminating that guilt," he writes.[12]

He suggests, moreover, that guilt and the God experience may be so connected that when one cannot authentically experience guilt, one cannot experience God. He writes: "I have met many men in the course of my life who have told me how, acting from high conscience as men who had become guilty [i.e., owned their guilt], they experienced themselves as seized by a higher power."[13]

To torment and harass yourself with guilt feelings over irrelevant and neurotic actions is to live in the "lowlands" of guilt, which serves as a camouflage for taking real relationship to one's own being.

To distinguish one's neurotic and problematic guilt from authentic guilt (where we do unto someone what we wouldn't want done to us) demands three courageous steps.

First, it demands the courage of "self-illumination." I let myself really feel the injury I have done another. Buber calls it the "shudder" of self-illumination.

Secondly, it requires the courage to own that though perhaps years have passed since I injured the other, I am still the same person who did the harm. I "persevere in identity with the act."

Thirdly, it requires the courage to repair the injury, to make "at-one-ment," whether to the person involved, if possible, or to others, if not.

Consolingly, he says, "The wounds of the order of being can be healed in infinitely many other places than those at which they were inflicted."[14]

I quote Buber at some length because he has been a guide for me in seeing the positive role that owning one's guilt can play in spiritual growth. Because I grew up a Snow White, rather easily conforming to outer laws, it has been hard for me to grow into the maturity of owning my sinfulness, to see the real destructiveness I can create. Until you can *feel* your sinfulness, your capacity for destruction, it is hard to feel other than a victim of other peoples' evil, and it is harder to relate to Jesus, who says very explicitly that He came to save sinners.

Why is there so much unclaimed evil in the world when 90 percent, I imagine, of any population would see themselves as "good" people. "I didn't do it" or "everybody was doing it" is not just the cry of a Richard Nixon of Watergate or a Lieutenant Calley of the My Lai massacre, but it is our general reaction to accusations of guilt. And so we live in the isolation of our thinly wrought righteousness and far from the Father who would run from afar to greet us at the slightest murmur. "Father, I have sinned before heaven and Thee; I am not worthy to be Thy child."

Think of the last time that someone, anyone, confessed their guilt to you and asked pardon. When did *you* last do that, not with a shallow "I'm sorry" but from a consciousness that you—that I—carry real responsibility for the enormous evil that threatens to inundate the world? If, as Jesus said, "The kingdom is within," so must the evil be within. And we can only be a part of the building of God's kingdom when we own—on a daily basis, as we ask for daily bread—our daily sinfulness.

During the first week of the thirty-day retreat, St. Ignatius would have the retreatant meditate on sin. I remember once thinking, Could I meditate for seven hours a day for seven days, forty-nine hours all told, on sin? God led me gently and directly and centrally to a scene that occured when I was thirteen years old, a very good girl: A family member is sobbing. I don't know what to do. I am thinking, She shouldn't be telling me this; I can't help. I shouldn't have to put up with this mess. I remain stone cold and leave her sobbing in her room.

Through the years I had remembered the scene as an example of my victimhood in being part of a family that never had its act together. The grace, the "shudder of self-illumination," came with the thought: Even a dog would have licked her hand. At that moment I owned my responsibility for the burden of sinfulness that my family, that every family, bears, and I was freed.

My major sin then, as it is now (and with grace I try to "persevere in identity" with that thirteen-year-old), was to choose isolation and fear over reaching out, not to save her—for rarely can we save anyone from pain—but to share the pain. As Buber says: "Each of us is encased in an armor which says 'You are not addressed; all is quiet.' Original guilt consists in remaining with oneself. If the being before whom this hour places one is not met with the truth of one's whole life, then one is guilty."[15]

Hard words, but not too hard for us, encased in our "sinless" armor—our immaculate deception which isolates us from God and man.

I do not want to leave you with insights with which to harass yourself, but with the conviction that the conversion experience, strangely reversed in our time, wherein we convert from blamelessness to owning our sinfulness, is a most freeing experience, unique in its access to the fathering, forgiving God whom Jesus calls *Abba*.

For Personal Reflection

1. Do you think there is a connection between the ability to own one's guilt and to experience God? Have you ever felt God's presence when you confessed your sin to yourself or another?
2. What are your favorite things to feel guilty about? Make a "harassment" list and then evaluate whether you live in the "highlands" or the "lowlands" of guilt.
3. Recall any memory you have of feeling the "shudder of self-illumination," when you had the courage to feel the pain you inflicted on another.
4. List those times in your life when you have relatively freely and deliberately done unto someone what you wouldn't want done unto you. Write one memory in detail; ask that person's pardon in written dialogue at least, or personally if you so discern that this would be beneficial to both. Ask Jesus to be your advocate if it is painful to own your pain.
5. When was the last time anyone begged your pardon for an injury? When you begged someone's pardon? Is it hard for you to make atonement?
6. Recall the kinds of things you have done in atonement for sins.
7. Has it been easy or difficult for you to claim your sinfulness?
8. List those people who have injured you. Dialogue with each until you feel forgiveness for their sin, and tell them so.

And Forgive Us Our Trespasses As We Forgive Those Who Trespass Against Us

DON BRIEL

Luther is said to have stated rather forcefully: "Sin powerfully; God can forgive only a hearty sinner." What perhaps strikes us to-day as so enigmatic in this passage of the Our Father is not God's capacity for forgiveness but rather our need for it in the first place. I was reminded of this recently while watching the television pre-sentation of *Brideshead Revisited*. One of the episodes seems to have produced not so much a debate among viewers about the source and implications of Julia's decision to break off her relation-ship with Charles because its continuance would have been sinful, but rather simple incredulity that something as natural as passion and as attractive as love could be seen to be sinful in the first place. The consensus seems to be that Julia would have have been well-advised to consult a therapist.

We have in large measure lost an awareness of sin, and though we may often feel the need for forgiveness, we rarely seem to know what it is for which we wish to be forgiven, except a general sense of inadequacy. It seems to me that the confusion on this point is demonstrative of the larger ethical problem of our time. Recogniz-ing the extent of our self-deception, we take for granted that all of our moral decision making is necessarily flawed and therefore can only be measured against the quality of awareness out of which we operated at that particular moment. All moral choices then are decisively and finally personal, and cannot be evaluated with ref-erence to any other standard of judgment. And so morality is re-duced to a tolerance of diversity and a compassion for our mutual weakness.

We are no longer called to confront the problem of evil, and we can dismiss its more obvious manifestations as symptoms of insan-ity. In such a world, the idea of forgiveness is meaningless. Who could presume to forgive or to ask for forgiveness of another? To do so would be to deny oneself in the name of another. We would simply be asking to be forgiven our humanity. At the least, such an appeal for forgiveness would seem artificial, at most perhaps dishonest.

We tend to focus on the rightness or wrongness of a personal act of moral decision making rather than on a quality of life. But in doing so we involve ourselves in a quagmire. As Stanley Hauerwas has said, "The moral life and ethics is distorted when we attempt to begin with the question 'What should I do in situation X or Y?' For to ask such a question gives the impression that situations can be abstracted, dealt with separate from their narrative context. But a situation is only such because of a particular kind of history."[16]

It is Hauerwas's contention that seeing truthfully involves a process of conversion in which we are tutored to a new awareness in accepting participation in the larger Christian story. In this context the fact that all of our decisions are in themselves at least partially flawed does not constitute an obstacle to living a moral life.

What is demanded is a realization that a moral life is not composed either of a series of decisions that are self-authenticating or of a model life, but of both together in a complex relationship by which lives are tutored by the Christian story and the story itself brought to life in our living it out in a series of choices.

From this point of view the contemporary religious crisis is not primarily intellectual at all. We are not so much concerned with the truth of statements about the existence of God or the divinity of Christ as we are with discovering anew a world in which such statements might make a difference, might be realized.

The crisis then is rather one of the imagination. We have lost the capacity to see how one idea, one symbol, one fact is related to another in a quality of tension that constitutes a field of force in which the truth is seen as a whole rather than in its parts. Instead we see things in isolation from one another, and our investigation of them, no matter how rigorous, is inevitably unsatisfactory. In fact, the more rigorous such investigations are, the less satisfactory they seem.

We have in our own time a peculiar desire for control, the need to "name things." Robert Coles said that "if anyone is given to naming, it is educated secular liberals—and a seer of sorts for many such people is the social scientist. We hunger for information, and often confuse what we find with final explanations of the very meaning of life."[17] What we have lost is a vital power of imaginatively perceiving things in their hidden wholeness.

We ignore what Virginia Woolf called the "vast, the general question" of the meaning of life and preoccupy ourselves with the facts of our existence, of the present condition of our identity. Is it any wonder that the chief metaphors of American life are medical? In what other age, what other culture, could one hear the statement that "as long as you have your health, you have everything" without a sense of shame?

In all of this we recognize that our sense of the value and dignity of human life has been reduced. Our moral decisions are pragmatic, utilitarian, and private. We make decisions about nuclear arms, abortion, or the distribution of human resources practically, based on current information; but there is no vital, integrating principle which might draw these various moral situations into a world of meaning. We have come to see the information itself as reliable only when it is removed from our own influence and interpretation. We seek the raw data, but this, too, only further alienates us from the truth that we seek to know. It is perhaps true in such a climate to speak of increased selfishness, but at the same time Camus may well have been correct in suggesting that the chronic problem of our time is not sin, not immorality, but boredom. Our age could well be summarized in his line: "We fornicated and read the papers." Kierkegaard had said much the same thing of the nineteenth century:

> Let others complain that the age is wicked; my complaint is that it lacks passion. Men's thoughts are flimsy like lace, they are themselves pitiable like the lacemakers. The thoughts of their hearts are too paltry to be sinful. For a worm it might be regarded as a sin to harbour such thoughts but not for a being made in the image of God. Their hearts are dull and sluggish, their passions sleepy. . . . This is the reason my soul al-

ways turns back to the Old Testament and to Shakespeare; I feel that those who speak there are at least human beings: they hate, they love, they murder their enemies, and curse their descendents through all generations: they sin.[18]

This awareness is not a new one. It is part of a larger Christian inheritance. Dante reminded us that the vast majority of human persons are neither moral nor immoral but are what he called the "trimmers." Neither hot nor cold, they abandon themselves neither to God nor to the devil, but to themselves. We are not so much drawn to the call of sanctity or of sinfulness as we are to the soft and indolent sound of our own voice. We rest in ourselves and find ourselves bored.

When Newman said that calculation never made a hero, he was warning us against an artificially intellectual explanation of life, but he was at the same time pointing to an unnerving truth: that Christianity and heroism are inextricably linked. In reading the New Testament, one of the most startling facts to me is that those who rejected Christ were uniformly correct, their passions contained. They were in control of their lives, their hearts, their minds. They were incorruptible because they were incapable of being seduced. But here is another curious paradox of Christianity. Only those who can be seduced by sin can be saved by God. So often as trimmers we spend our lives in seducing ourselves.

I remember as a freshman in an English composition course at Notre Dame being asked to write an essay on a sonnet which I did not recognize as John Donne's. As a class, we unanimously condemned it; the author lacked courage, we said. He should have assumed a greater degree of responsibility for his own actions if he sought to claim a religious identity.

I have forgotten the instructor's name, but I haven't forgotten his anger at our response. He was not a Catholic, rare enough in those days of the mid-sixties at Notre Dame, and he said the the self-satisfaction and complacency of our papers seemed to demonstrate minds more or less impervious to the appeal of Christianity. To some extent he was wrong. We were perhaps impervious to humility. We were not completely impervious to a kind of heroism, but what we did not know was that Christian heroism is inevitably humble, and so John Donne's lines speak not of a coward but of the saint:

> Batter my heart, three person'd God; for, you
> As yet but knocke, breathe, shine, and seeke to mend;
> That I may rise, and stand, o'erthrow mee, 'and bend
> Your force, to breake, blowe, burn and make me new.
> I, like an usurpt towne, to 'another due,
> Labour to 'admit you, but Oh, to no end,
> Reason your viceroy in mee, mee should defend,
> But is captiv'd, and proves weake or untrue,
> Yet dearely 'I love you, and would be lov'd faine,
> But am betroth'd unto your enemie,
> Divorce mee, 'untie, or breake that knot againe,
> Take mee to you, imprison mee, for I
> Except you 'enthrall mee, never shall be free,
> Nor ever chast, except you ravish mee.

There is a peculiar proximity of sanctity to sinfulness. Its frequent appearance in Christian literature has led to any number of oversimplifications about Catholic preoccupation with gloom or unworldly joy. There is as well a peculiar closeness between pain and joy, and it is not merely that each is characterized by a certain intensity.

St. Augustine thought that the greatest cure for pride was a "broad and disgraceful sin" and implied that because we are all so proud, the experience of sin is a necessary means to conversion.

But if sin itself has disappeared, so too has the opportunity for conversion. We remain in our isolation, less and less splendid, more and more deformed. When *Love Story* told us that love means never having to say you're sorry, it undoubtedly expressed a new understanding of love and one with a certain appeal, but it also pointed to a basic dilemma of our time: our incapacity to express our need for forgiveness and our unwillingness to forgive others. Instead we accept diversity. The cost of such impoverishing toleration is a more or less absolute alienation, for what we are finally admitting is that we no longer have anything in common that makes demands on how we live out who we are.

The Our Father reminds us of an alternative: that we are called to conversion; that we are called to forgiveness; that we are called to live out the Incarnation of Christ in transforming ourselves in His image, not through the power of our own courage, but in a costly and humble heroism in which we allow ourselves to be seduced even by the Father.

For Personal Reflection

1. List those times in your life when you felt the Lord calling you to conversion of your ways? Write out one of these in detail.
2. What do you feel is the central sin and fear the Lord is asking you to let go of?
3. When have you ever used psychological excuses rather than owning your sin? When have you been aware of another person doing this?
4. Which part of your life story do you feel is the most Christian? What is most flawed by illusion and excuse? Read this to a good friend and ask him or her for a reaction.
5. Write a response to the John Donne poem.
6. When has your pride ever been cured by a broad and disgraceful sin?

And Forgive Us Our Trespasses As We Forgive Those Who Trespass Against Us

RONDA CHERVIN

This word *forgiveness* touches me so deeply I feel I must start with an image rather than a concept.

There was a fatherly priest I loved tenderly. He had ministered Christ's forgiveness to me in times of desperate need. At a prayer meeting he was laying hands over a long line of people. I was called to assist by joining another woman to hold them and pray with them as they kneeled. From that close proximity I was able to observe the face and gestures of Father T. in a different way than when I was penitent.

I discovered that he touched each person according to individual need, laying his hand lightly on a highly coiffed head, in a hard brotherly grasp on middle-aged men's shoulders, with special warmth on the less beautiful women, with reverent space for the normally flirtatious.

I was overwhelmed at the thought that despite the number in the crowd, this leader, who rarely speaks of psychology but only of universal spiritual themes, could instinctively know how to touch each person, and what is more, how to pour out the words each needed to hear.

Now came the moment I dreaded. Way back at the end of the line I had noticed a woman I could not forgive. Secretly I hoped that she would leave, unwilling to wait so long for her blessing. But now she was advancing closer and closer. She knelt most humbly, bowing her head without a word to indicate the nature of her need. The priest I thought of as *my* priest gazed down at this other woman with a look of absolute tender mercy. As he stretched out his arm in a gesture like that of Jesus in the raising of Lazarus as painted by Rembrandt, grace flooded his countenance. I saw him as Jesus saving, and her, my "enemy," as an archetype of all forgiven souls. She left the church. I wept and wept for my hardness of heart and the miracle of having seen how the Father loved us both through the mediation of His priest. The Father who sent His Son, not to condemn, but to redeem.

Another image comes. In a book about the lives of the Desert Fathers by Helen Waddell there is a story of an old hermit who adopted a young girl orphan and raised her to be his successor. All went well until one day a traveler passed, fell in love with the girl, and seduced her. Horrified and ashamed, she fled to the city without speaking to her aged mentor. Years later, learning that his long-mourned spiritual daughter had become a prostitute, the ancient monk traveled to the city, disguised himself, and came to her as a patron. Once in her tent he removed the disguise and, weeping, begged her to return. Stunned at the forgiveness of the "father" she had imagined to have rejected her totally, she went back to the desert and became a holy woman.

This story was read to me by a monk during the rite of confession at a moment when I despaired of forgiveness. Afterwards I rose from my knees, feeling myself a new woman. For many years I had striven and struggled and flagellated myself, hoping to become a saint. Now I had failed totally, and in the darkest moment I discovered that the Father loved me the more, as He sent one of His human emissaries to rescue me from my pit. "My love for Him had been but a shadow of His love for me."

At a large charismatic convention in Albuquerque whose theme was "Forgive and You Shall Be Forgiven," the image was given of each of the three thousand people attending as a circle of a particular color. Each circle was separate from the others. It was said that once we had forgiven each other from the heart, we would become one big circle, the light would be radiant, and in our oneness we would know the Father's forgiveness. Heads bowed, hands joined, a leader called out different sins of others and of ourselves which we might forgive or ask forgiveness for. The ones whose hands we held were to symbolize our victims or victimizers, forgiving or forgiven. After many sins were mentioned, a Spanish-speaking leader got up impromptu and called for forgiveness for all the sins of racism. Waves of emotion shuddered through the mass of people, many of whom were of mixed descent. After many tears and reconciling embraces the music ministry played "And The Father Will Dance."

Joy broke loose as more and more of us joined the young people who had begun circle dances around the arena. I knew not a single person in the crowd as more than an acquaintance, yet I was drawn into a rapture of unity greater than I had ever experienced. Forgiveness had wiped away the tears. The tears had formed a river of love. The love had erupted into dance. At the very end the speaker arose and proclaimed, "Jesus was willing to die on the Cross because He knew what the joy of our reconciliation with the Father would be like — like this!"

It is astonishing how often Jesus mentions forgiveness. How well He understood that root of our hardness of heart. He must have been sickened by our resentments, the revenge plotted in the dark, the sneering satisfaction at the misfortunes of those who could have been our brothers and sisters. In parable after parable He tries to show us how unreasonable it is to see our own faults as so inoffensive and understandable, and those of others as malicious and worthy of total condemnation.

But how shall we move into the joy of forgiveness, we whose wounds are so deep, whose recriminations growl from the bottom of the unconscious, periodically to erupt in violent words and deeds?

Here are some paths toward forgiveness that have been healing for me. One is the method called "healing of memories." As a part of spiritual psychology, it consists in going back to the past in the realization that God was present at our worst moments and that if we go back to them in the spirit we can be healed of the pain of them.

In terms of forgiveness we can use the healing of memories technique in this way:[19] List the people you feel have hurt you the most. Taking them one by one, pray to understand what their own wounds were at the time they hurt you. See if you can see them, not as huge giants menacing you, but as troubled, struggling, unhappy people. Then try to see what good God brought out of the pain that came from this person's way of dealing with you. Can you forgive them, as Christ has forgiven you, for hurting others when you were too unhappy to give what they needed?

Another path toward forgiveness consists in identifying myself-as-victim with a time in the life of Christ when He experienced the same basic agony. Am I rejected by one I love? That is His basic sorrow. His loved ones—us—refuse the very love that could redeem them. Am I lonely? How lonely was He when He returned to His own village, only to be cast out; when in the Garden none of His disciples would stay up to comfort Him? Have my enemies caused me to fail? How did Jesus feel when condemned by the Sanhedrin?

Such meditations cannot be made superficially. We must take

our non-forgiveness seriously enough as a major barrier to salvation on heaven and on earth so that we will spend many hours uniting ourselves to Christ—just as long as it takes to cry out with sincerity, "Father, forgive them, they know not what they do."

"Hell is not being able to love," wrote George Bernanos. Our hearts shrink whenever we say that we can't forgive this one, or can never bear to see that one. No one with hate in his heart can be in heaven, for heaven is perfect love. So there is no shortcut. Either we refuse to forgive and make our hearts sink into hell; or we are purged in the fire until all the sludge is burned out; or we forgive now from the heart, preparing the way for the heavenly kingdom to come.

How strong are the words of the Psalmist:

> Blessed is he whose transgression is forgiven,
> whose sin is covered
>
> . . . .
>
> When I declared not my sin,
> my body wasted away,
> through my groaning all day long.
> For day and night
> thy hand was heavy upon me;
> my strength was dried up,
> as by the heat of summer."
>
> (Psalm 32:1–4)

> O Father, forgive, forgive, forgive
> and make forgiveness to flow from me
> that all may be one and our joy may be full
> *And the Father may dance*

For Personal Reflection

1. Describe some instances in your life of forgiveness of others, their forgiveness of you, and God's forgiveness.
2. Who are the people you think have most victimized you? Can you try a healing exercise or meditation to move toward reconciliation?

Chapter **6**

Meditations on Lead Us Not Into Temptation, but Deliver Us from Evil

And Lead Us Not into Temptation, but Deliver Us from Evil

MARY NEILL

† The Irish theologian James Mackey says of the Our Father that it "is simple to say and all but impossible to live." He goes on to explain that the crux of the difficulty comes from the fact that if we live it, we will be brought to the test. And so Jesus instructs us to pray that we not be led to this test, into temptation. Mackey says that

> the attempt to live out the experience of the reign of God in our lives will involve offence and persecution . . . and the last petition of the prayer is simply the request that the persecution may not come, or if it does, that we may come out of it with integrity, still faithful to our lived conviction that everyone is of equal value to God and intended to be equally graced with his gifts.[20]

Jesus instructs us in the Our Father that it is arrogant to search for suffering; certainly He never did. It came as a by-product of saying what He knew from the Father had to be said about the kingdom of God, knowing well that the "godly" men of this time would be mortally offended.

It is important to reflect on the centrality of not asking to be tempted because perhaps there has been, as Matthew Fox asserts, a certain focus toward *via negativa* spirituality in the Church for a long time. Those who see the story of creation as the story of the fall have been more dominant than those, many of them mystics, who see Genesis primarily as the story of blessing: "And God saw everything that He had made and behold it was very good" (Gen. 1:30).

If we deliberately exacerbate our suffering and seek persecution, perhaps semiconsciously we are not serving the kingdom but serving our own death instincts. We say, as it were, "Well, if suffering is the name of the game, I will seek it." And so we are warned by Jesus' instruction to Peter, "Pray that you enter not into temptation." We must pray that we not be brought to the test.

Jesus was put to the test and He passed; Peter was tested and failed. Judas was tested and lost his soul: "It were better for this man that he had not been born."

Jesus teaches us not to seek the testing, so terrible it can be, so frail is our weakness in that confusing whirlpool. The petition implies that God is not a "nice uncle"; it is He who can lead us to the test; it is He alone who can deliver us from its evil. The tests devised by the Lord are not to be lightly encountered or sought. "Even His mercy burns," Flannery O'Connor writes.

Have you ever wondered why courage is so rare, grace and wisdom such refreshing oddities in our age when even evil is banal?

I think it is because it is pain alone that teaches wisdom and few learn to bear well the deep pain that is the mother of deep wisdom. Courage is made strong in the school of suffering. "The office of love is to wound," says St. John of the Cross cryptically, implying that great lovers must endure great wounding. But woe to those who go to the test unprepared like Peter, who trusted in his own strength ("I will never deny you!"), or Judas, who trusted in money.

All of us, I imagine, have confidence in our powers of endurance, and a list of resources for hard times: people to call, books to read, prayers to say. We imagine that we can pass most tests, as we have become "test-wise" in our multiple-choice age. Think for a minute of just the academic tests you've taken in your lifetime; consider the many testings of your relationships, jobs, self-esteem. You could not be reading this book without having passed thousands of tests.

The danger, Jesus seems to imply, is that we can in our over-confidence be delivered to a testing so painful and hazardous that our survival is precarious, hanging on the thin thread of a faith that continues to believe even in the deepest darkness. Just as surely as Jesus was put to the test in His passion, so, surely, He prayed anxiously and acutely to be delivered from it. "Father, let this cup pass." Only through falling and crying out did He survive the Garden of Gethsemane, the road to Calvary, and cling in darkness to an Abba who willed His cruel death and suffering.

All of us can love a father that is kind and thoughtful, just as all can love our friends; it would seem to be a rare child who can not only cling to, but also come to love and forgive, an abusive parent. It is supernatural, a miracle of grace, for the child that can. All of us can love the image of the Prodigal Father, the father who cries out, "This is My beloved son on whom My favor rests." Fewer, far fewer, can love the Father of Calvary, all silence and darkness while His son suffers deepest abandonment. Only the most holy pass this test — to love God, not because He is "nice" and brings them to life, but because He is *God*. "Father and fondler of heart Thou hast wrung; hast Thy dark descending and most art merciful then" (Gerard Manley Hopkins).

This sense of being abandoned not just by all humanity but by God Himself seems the most painful of tests. In grieving at my father's death, feeling abandoned without his life, support, and comfort, I felt great anger, even hatred of God. What a terrible system! No wonder Woody Allen says cynically, "God is not evil; He's just an underachiever."

Then I let myself remember those times when I felt God had

abandoned me to suffer deep physical, psychological, or moral evil. Never deserving it, wanting it, willing it, I was submerged. I understood then why people can be so cruel to one another. One's sense of abandonment and outrage seems to justify indifference to others' pain because our own pain has been so lonely-making and constant while the Father of life has seemed so indifferent.

And yet to rest in this outraged consciousness is to live in the kingdom of evil, of the prince of liars who affirms, "God doesn't care at all—that's what you feel, isn't it? That's the *absolute truth*."

The temptation continues: If God has permitted me to suffer great evil, why should I break the chain of evil? And so perhaps at this dangerous place we can only pray over and over: "Deliver me from this evil. Deliver me from judging God, from calling Him to the test." As Job learned, those who test the Lord and call Him to an account will never get an answer.

We would all walk gladly with the Father in the Garden of Creation; we must be hesitant to go to the test of the Father on Calvary.

The ultimate question is: Can I love someone I don't understand? Can I love my best friend, myself when I don't understand and there's so much pain? Can I love a God I don't understand? As Flannery O'Connor poignantly writes:

> His head was churning with old rages. The afternoon he had learned the extent of Bishop's [his retarded child's] future had sprung to his mind. He saw himself rigidly facing the doctor, ... He had said, "You should be grateful his health is good. In addition to this, I've seen them born blind as well, some without arms and legs, and one with a heart outside."
>
> He had lurched up, almost ready to strike the man. "How can I be grateful," he had hissed, "when one—just one—is born with a heart outside?"
>
> "You'd better try," the doctor had said.
> (*The Violent Bear It Away* [New York: Signet, 1960], p.387)

I'd better try.

The God who brings us to the test by seeming to abandon us, so that perhaps we can learn that feeling abandoned is *being* abandoned, is a God whom we need to forgive for mysterious ways that include much darkness and pruning. Only one well-practiced in forgiveness can have compassion for God Himself and the limits imposed by the materials from which we were made — *blue nothing*. I don't know whether ontologically the evil I suffer from in life is God's permissive will or what. I only know that it hurts, and sooner or later I have to deal with that hurt as temptation to perpetuate personal evil.

Then, after taking my hurts seriously enough to own them and fight the temptation to cling to them, I may be ready to take seriously the sufferings of God in the world. This description of Dietrich Bonhoeffer in his last days offers a vision of a man who has passed the last test:

> The struggle to abandon to God his rich and treasured past, the struggle with the last vestiges of his pride, the struggle to suffer, in full measure and yet in gratitude, his human longings in the midst of his own pain; all this had led him to that experience of the Cross, in which at last, through a grasp of reality so intense that it fused all the elements of his being into a single whole, he learnt what life can be when "we throw ourselves completely into the arms of God, taking seriously not our own sufferings, but the sufferings of God in the world."[21]

For Personal Reflection

1. List the times in your life when you have been put to the test. Describe one in some detail and then write a reflection on testing.
2. When have you put others to the test?
3. Have you ever experienced outrage at God for what seems unjust suffering? (If you haven't, read the Book of Job and the Book of Jonas and hear their complaints.) Write a dialogue with God about this anger.
4. Has your anger ever been so great that you could call it hatred of God? Have you ever known anyone to express hatred of God's

ways? How did you feel when this happened? Macmurray says that "hatred is inevitable in all relationships." Do you think one's relationship with God should be exempted from this generalization?

5. Remember a time when you were indifferent and cruel in face of another's pain. How did your own pain play a part in this scene?

And Lead Us Not into Temptation, but Deliver Us from Evil

DON BRIEL

So often in our own time we emphasize the necessity for self-improvement; we speak of the need to choose the good in life, we seek to discover. As Americans especially, we are tempted to live out of a frontier mentality in which we might function as pioneers, imposing a new order on the unstructured, unsettled territory of life. In this we emphasize our need to create. We honor those who have influenced events, who are steely-eyed, who have created new worlds.

Again we tend to link freedom and power as correlative realities. The liberated woman is freed in the sense that she is capable of exercising independence, which means that she exercises power, that she makes a difference. This is a simple equation, and it may well be true that D. H. Lawrence was right in suggesting that this purely negative definition of freedom, so prevalent in American history, is merely a rattling of chains.

If we speak of freedom merely as an absence of restraint, then truly free persons are those who live in radical separation from others, operating only from a position of power. This is part of a long tradition of American heroism, set almost exclusively in the vast unsettled lands of the wild West. American heroes are strong and independent and rootless. Why are there no American heroes in Cleveland or Newark?

96

Freedom, like any other virtue, cannot, without serious distortion, be reduced to a single vision. A definition of freedom makes sense only in relation to other virtues. One must ask, "Freed for what; freed to what?" Freedom so understood may well not be an end in itself but a means to, and a part of, a larger integrated human life. But this raises the need for a much larger question about what it means to live out a fully human existence in the first place.

It is interesting to note that the current television series of the same name portrays the greatest American hero as one who has received his heroic powers from an extraterrestrial source. He has not earned such a grace except insofar as he shows a general goodwill and a defined compassion for others. His exercise of these powers is somewhat chaotic because he has lost the directions that accompanied them. He works in a vital interdependence with people about whom he is concerned, and the relationships with them define him as a person. Finally, in order to determine the value of his use of these powers, the viewer is compelled to bring to bear a larger world of reference. This new understanding is much closer to classical models of heroism, but our culture as a whole is not yet fully aware of the possibilities of this humbler and more complex heroic vision.

This thought or truth reminds us of a fundamental religious insight. The decisive choice is not ours but God's. We define ourselves as God's people because we have been chosen, not because we choose. In this sense, all of religious life is a creative, active response to the burden of being loved, of being graced, of having been chosen. The truly terrifying thing about life is that it is not what we make it.

As we see so often in Flannery O'Connor's fiction and in our own world of terror, grace is everywhere, and quoting Teilhard, she reminds us that "everything that rises must converge."

There are events and persons in our lives which we encounter seemingly accidentally, but which decisively challenge our perception of what is true and confront us with the possibility of conversion. Curiously all grace is apparently accidental, but these accidental occasions of grace are not simply the passive clay awaiting creative hands. Freedom is not found simply by exercising control over events and persons, but in discovering a deepened perception of who we are as persons engaged in our own history, engaged in the history of others. We are freed in this way, not only to a heightened awareness of our identity, but also to action, to a capacity for living out that awareness.

In this sense, life is not simply the raw material for fashioning an independent identity or purpose in order to reassure us of our own existence, but is a fundamental mystery in which we struggle for an integrated vision of what is real. There is the need for a constant shifting of perspective, for what John Coulson calls the "stereoscopic vision" in which we both recognize our obligation to exercise a degree of autonomy and at the same time realize our dependence on others, on God. There is a necessary tension here in which we decisively choose ourselves and come to recognize our participation in a pattern of meaning that cannot be reduced to our own construct.

We are peculiarly "middle" creatures. Life is neither meaningful nor meaningless. It is both at the same time. We tend to think that life is composed either of decisive choices which define us or of no choices at all. We either insist on our creative self-definition or take a kind of drab comfort in the apparently haphazard quality of our lives, of our experience, and emphasize our limited capacity for influencing events or concerning ourselves with their implications.

There is a comfort, cold perhaps, in the latter view of our helplessness as well as in the view that life's significance is self-contained, self-conferred. They are in one way remarkably alike. In each case, we are trapped in ourselves.

The Our Father radically reasserts that human life is exercised neither autonomously nor accidentally. There are decisive tests of our humanity, which we are unable to confront unaided, except in a kind of tragedy. At the same time, we recognize that life abounds with trials, with temptations, and so we tend to pray the lines as if we expect the temptations, but hope to be spared their consequences. In Paul's letter to Timothy, however, we are told that temptation itself must finally be avoided:

> Those who want to be rich are falling into temptation and a
> trap. They are letting themselves be captured by foolish and
> harmful desires which drag men down to ruin and destruc-
> tion. The love of money is the root of all evil. Some men in
> their passion for it have strayed from the faith, and have
> come to grief among great pain.

Here, too, we see our dependence on the Father, but this dependence is complex. We do not seek to avoid the effects of unavoid-
able trials; rather, we pray to the Father, asking that our wills be
animated so as to choose Him, to choose the good absolutely. We
need to remind ourselves that choices do not occur in a vacuum,
they occur only in the context of a relationship. The idea of a sov-
ereign, independent movement of the will is illusion, but so too is
the idea that no such positive movement is possible.

In Luke's Gospel, Jesus tells us, "What father among you will
give his son a snake if he asks for a fish, or hand him a scorpion if he
asks for an egg? If you with all your sins know how to give your children good things, how much more will the heavenly Father give
the Holy Spirit to those who ask Him?" The analogy is helpful and
shows how clear is the need to go beyond the loving concern of the
earthly father to the knowledge of the Heavenly Father. As an
earthly father, the Holy Spirit is not mine to give. I often wonder
how clearly I have been able to discriminate between the fish and
the snake, between the egg and the scorpion.

What do we really offer our children? From what temptations
do we seek to protect them? I try to protect them from the more
squalid temptations of life, but I do know as well that the great
temptations of life are rarely merely squalid; they possess a certain
dignity.

More directly, I would like to protect my children from an uncri-
ticized life, from cynicism, but most importantly from the single vision, which reduces life and ignores the inherent interdependence,
complexity, and wholeness of human existence in vital relation to
the Father. In all of this we see darkly, and the answer is not ours
alone. As a father, my best hope is that my children might see in me
a reflection, however lambently, of the Father's love for them.

For Personal Reflection

1. What is your image of the hero; of yourself as hero or heroine? How does it correspond to the American image; the image of the saints?
2. What elements in your life do you see as accidental and which chosen by you or God? How does your labeling affect your ultimate judgment of these events?
3. Which temptations in your life do you see as being or having been squalid and which ennobling?

And Lead Us Not into Temptation, but Deliver Us from Evil

RONDA CHERVIN

I have heard that some Scripture scholars say that the real meaning of this phrase is "Postpone the Day of Judgment." But since the older translation is so much a part of the history of spirituality and of parish homilies, it seems more fruitful to meditate on that related meaning: that we pray that the Lord not let us be tempted and that He deliver us from the evil that threatens us physically, mentally, and spiritually.

When I think of temptation I recall Satan's forty-day trial of Jesus in the desert and I want to see how those enigmatic words might apply to my own trials.

"And the tempter came and said to him, 'If you are the Son of God, command these stones to become loaves of bread'" (Matt. 4:3). It sounds so reasonable to me. After so many days and nights of struggle, why shouldn't God turn the stony hearts of my adversaries, my students, my teenagers into the nice warm bread of mutual love and respect? If God won't do it at my bidding, I turn without realizing it to the ways of the Evil One. I will make my adversaries come over to my side by cracking the rock of their arguments with the sword of logic. I will force my students to respond to my power as their professor. I will win over my teenagers by extravagant gestures, or by shame, so that they will give up their freedom and become dough in my hands once again.

But Jesus said, "Man does not live by bread alone but by the Father's will." If it not yet be the Father's will to turn my stones into bread, shall I not trust my desert fast as purification and offer my trials as intercession?

> Then the devil took him to the holy city, and set him on the pinnacle of the temple and said to him, "If you are the Son of God, throw yourself down; for it is written, 'He will give his angels charge of you and on their hands they will bear you up, let you strike your foot against a stone.'" (Matt. 4:5-6)

For me this image represents the temptation to throw myself down from the positions God has given me, which seem like very unpleasant places to be at times, and instead to fly through the air on fantasy trips. Why stay at my university? Why not give it all up and perhaps God will make me into a contemplative mystic instead, held up by angels alone! Why stay with my family? Why not instead join a community of ardent Christians sharing the utopian life? God can take care of the family in some other way. But Jesus said, "You shall not tempt the Lord your God" (Matt. 4:7). When had the Father told me that I should leave my clear duty for Elysian fields of my imagination?

Again, the devil took Him to a very high mountain and showed Him all the kingdoms of the world and the glory of them, and he said to Him, "All these I will give you, if you will fall down and worship me."

For me this image conveys the possibility that if I became assertive and powerful, and if I could call the shots instead of being subordinate and vulnerable to the vexing will of others, I could insist that everyone do just what I know is best and then the kingdom of heaven shall come for us. Why shouldn't I be the boss of the family? Why shouldn't I run the university in my image? Then I could fire my enemies and hire my friends, choose ideal students, and it would be paradise. Why shouldn't I run the parish and put in all the innovations I know would work?

But Jesus said, "You shall worship the Lord your God and Him only shall you serve." Awful! Continue to be a servant instead of the master? Accept the roles I have been given? Worship God with humble heart instead of being the central figure myself, to be adored as savior of the family, the university, the parish? Yes! Groan . . .

Many of the Jews rejected the Son of God because He came as a suffering servant. In the desert was His great chance to become the leader they wanted. He rejected it in sheer obedience and love for the Father's plan, no matter what the cost. Shall I not follow?

Is there really a choice? The devil is the father of all lies. Taking up his offers leads nowhere. In fact, it leads to the evils from which Jesus tells us to pray for deliverance. Trying to get my own way leads to despair and finally fantasies of suicide. The devil wants our destruction. Trying to get my own way leads to rage, the desire to kill literally or figuratively those who will not go along. Trying to get my own way leads to discouraged hopelessness.

"If you would be my disciple, take up your cross and follow me." Jesus does not mind if we tremble, try to flee. He understands. "Father, if thou wilt, take this chalice away from me." But He longs for us to come to Him in trial that He might strengthen us with the gifts of the Spirit, with the companionship of our brothers and sisters, that we might do the will of the Father with gladness. As soon as I return to Him, my burdens seem light, my yoke easy. I see myself and my family, and my students, and my opponents as funny creatures. I cherish the moments of breakthrough, ready to lay down my life for the goodness that surfaces amidst the ambiguity.

The Psalmist declares: "He delivered me, because He delighted in me."[22] What a splendid joyful vision of the Father's love.

> O Father, my father,
> lead me not to the trial
> strengthen me with your Spirit
> for someday we will drink the chalice of salvation together
> *And the Father will dance.*

For Personal Reflection

1. What are the "stones" in your life? Are you tempted to use illegitimate methods to turn them to bread?
2. What hard places do you want to escape from, hoping to fly through the air carried by angels?
3. What ruling position in family, job, community do you seek in a wrong spirit? Can you accept the servant role when necessary?
4. What have been the moments you were most threatened by evils without or within? How has Jesus stood by you in battle?

Chapter **7**

Meditations on For Thine Is the Kingdom and the Power and the Glory Forever

For Thine Is the Kingdom, and the Power, and the Glory Forever

MARY NEILL

☩ The Our Father is not a "pretty" prayer, and it has become clearer to me why it has not been my favorite. Is it your favorite prayer or that of anyone you know?

> First, the prayer attacks:
> —our isolation, which would say "my wife, my house, my dog, *my* Father in heaven";
> —our ingratitude and cursing, our complacency about holiness—ours and God's;
> —our desire to rule our own lives, to work for our own "kingship";
> —our self-will and laziness. "May my will be done on earth and God worry about heaven" might more accurately be our prayer stance.

Then it exposes:

—our hunger (daily and urgent) for physical and spiritual feeding and our inadequacy in keeping food supplies filled;

—our sinfulness, our every-day-this-day complicity with destruction;

—our unwillingness to forgive God and man for any injuries received;

—our weakness in the face of evil: our blind self-confidence, which is hazardous.

This is the "bad news" aspect of the Our Father, and it takes great holiness and simplicity to say, "Well, Jesus is right. These are the things that must be taken from me before I can have His consciousness of God as Abba!" Kierkegaard notes that, "God *took* Eve from Adam's side, because community first takes from you, before it gives."

Jesus, true friend, would help us take away the illusions that prevent us from seeing his Father. "And when you light a lamp you will see him" (Robert Bly).

What is the "good news" of the Our Father? That deliverance is possible. Jesus' assault on heaven is direct and imperative: COME, DO, GIVE, FORGIVE, LEAD NOT, DELIVER. He *commands* the Father. It's one thing to command the storm, but to command the Father of the storm? He teaches us to command God. We have access to His power; we need not despair when our weakness and hollowness and sinfulness abound. "His strength abounds in our weakness."

So it is fitting that the early Christians, aware that humility was their treasure, added this acclamation:

> For Thine is the kingdom,
> the power,
> and the glory.

"Not to us, not to us give glory, but to Yourself. For You alone are lord, You alone are God, You alone are most high."

For Thine Is the Kingdom, and the Power, and the Glory Forever

DON BRIEL

Charles Davis has said that the principal purpose of language is to mediate our experience and that because we no longer experience life hierarchically, the symbolism of the Our Father no longer makes sense. The Our Father presupposes, he wrote, "a set of social relationships no longer ours today: without patriarchy, fatherhood does not evoke transcendence; the name of rulers are not exalted, save in some survival of archaic ceremonial; kingly rule as such is no longer a reality; society is not an affair of a single will, but of consensus; we consider we have a right to the necessities of life and do not need to ask for them as a bounty.[23] Because we experience life in a radically different way, the contemporary need is not for theologians and commentators on the old images, but rather for poets who might replace the old images with new ones which more closely correspond to our present experience.

In an apt example, Davis points to a fact that is commonplace. In Christian worship the reality of God is rarely experienced. Because we have no "experienced images," we fill our liturgies with talk about community and personal worth, with what Davis calls idle chatter because there is no sustaining vision of the reality of God which might make such a sense of community and personal value capable of being realized.

Our liturgies are rarely characterized by reverence because it is not the reality of God that evokes our religious expression; it is rather our need for religious self-expression. In all of this there is no little artifice and frustration. The only solution, according to Davis, is to discover the new images which might enable us to restore our experience of the reality of God.

But in one sense Davis overemphasizes one pole of this mediating role of language at the expense of the other; the function of language is not merely to express one's experience but also to tutor it. We come to know who our fathers are, not merely through our immediate experience of them, but also by forming a general impression of the series of images which evoke the meaning of the word *father* and then by interpreting our own fathers' lives in the light of this general impression.

What we know as true about fatherhood is in one sense the product of a conversation between the experiences we have and the language we use to describe them. In this our experience alone is not decisive. The language of the Our Father trains us to see reality in a new way, and its claims to be true can only be tested in living out the vision which it reveals. This testing occurs in an ongoing tension between our experience and the words employed, each giving life and meaning to the other.

In this sense, the Our Father is the central prayer of Christianity less because it defines the Father than because it defines our relationship with Him and with one another; but this is a relationship which is rarely perceived in our own time. We tend to reduce the truths of life, of literature, and of religion to a simple statement, a private interpretation.

When we read a novel we look for the hero who tells the truth, the character with whom we identify. The other characters merely serve as foils to this protagonist, and we tend to see our own lives as truth-tellers in a similar way. We are preoccupied with personal integrity. Although this is not new, the idea that the truth is told singularly is in one sense a peculiarly modern illusion.

All good works of fiction are convincingly realistic because they resist the single interpretation which reduces life to a theory. The truth of any novel is demonstrated in a complex series of apparently contradictory but nonetheless interdependent speech and action in which no character tells the truth, though all may be truth-tellers. The fact is that truth is perceived only in a unity of apprehension in which we hold a whole series of characters and actions in our mind at once and thus are able to interpret their significance in relation to each other. This characteristic of fiction is not unrelated to a distinctive quality of Christian life in which we cannot entirely separate our awareness of ourselves from the community of persons made one in Christ.

It is in this sense that the most terrible line of the Bible is Cain's "Am I my brother's keeper?" To define oneself as a Christian is to accept a common identity in which one's singularity is neither reduced nor relieved, but rather in the vital tension that such a vision of life suggests: suffering and responsibility are in one sense interchangeable terms. What it means to be a Christian is realized in the relation of each to all; it is to live out, as did the Son, that paradoxical expression of the Father's love in the Incarnation.

To pray the Our Father is to commit ourselves to a life of interdependence and struggle and suffering in which to find our life is to lose it and in which the sustaining images draw us into a relationship that is personal but never private. There is in all of this an element of tragedy because what is real is beyond our capacity to control, to construct. But for the Christian, it is not the tragic element which is decisive; it is rather the love of the Father, which makes all things new.

For Personal Reflection

1. How does the Our Father, drawing on your own memory of or participation in fatherhood, tutor you to understand God in new ways?
2. How does the fatherhood of God encourage us to see things "whole" rather than in isolation? Have you experienced this as a central task of fathers?
3. In what way is it true that to pray the Our Father is to commit oneself to a new understanding of life?

For Thine Is the Kingdom, and the Power, and the Glory Forever

RONDA CHERVIN

I imagine Jesus enunciating the Great Prayer for all ages, then pausing a second and hearing all the human "But, but, but, not yet, not yet, not yet," and then to win us over adding sharply and thrillingly, "For Thine is the kingdom, and the power, and the glory forever." Those images must have elated a people who had waited for centuries for the coming of the kingdom, the power, and the glory.

Forever, everlasting, eternal. How can we be so myopic as to limit our vision of the earth — we whose Father is eternal, we to whom the Son proclaims an everlasting kingdom, we to whom the Holy Spirit has given the first fruits of the glory? How vital it is to ponder the Scriptures, to feed ourselves on the words of life of the fathers and mothers of the Church, the prophets, the teachers, the saints, lest we let ourselves be dragged down by dreary images of death.

In every life, our spiritual guides tell us, there is the purgation, where we are cleansed by the stinging medicaments from the infection that oozes out of the wounds of the past. In every life there is a time of illumination when the splendid vision of the kingdom floats above us yet is unable to penetrate the thick matrix of our daily duties. In every life, however, there is the possibility of the time of unity, when in surrender we give up all our self-redemptive schemes and make ourselves into clay in the Father's hands, that He may fashion us into peaceful, tender, ardent, humorous, committed doers of the Word.

> And the Father will dance
> when we know he is Our Father
> when we praise His name
> when we long for His Kingdom
> when we do His will
> when we forgive and are forgiven
> when He brings us victorious through temptation
> when He delivers us from evil
> and the Father will dance
> as on a day of joy
> He will exult over us
> And renew us in His Love.

110

For Personal Reflection

1. Write down new understandings of the Father which have come to you from reflecting on the Our Father.
2. What is the Father's central gift to you?
3. What is the central task you hear Him calling you to?
4. What (who) shall be your help in answering the call?
5. Recite the Our Father over slowly again and again, hearing its call and comfort. Then recite your favorite prayer and note what contrasts there are.
6. Make up an "Our Father" that speaks to you where you are right now in your journey from isolation and pain to joyful transcendence.

Notes

1. Marie-Louise von Franz, *The Passion of Perpetua* (Irving, Texas: Spring Publications, 1980), p. 10.
2. Paul Tillich, *The Shaking of the Foundations* (New York: Charles Scribner's Sons, 1948), p. 136.
3. John Dunne, *A Search for God in Time and Memory* (New York: Macmillan Co., 1969), p. 109.
4. For an account of my conversion see *The Church of Love* (originally published by Liguori; now available from Chiaro-Oscuro Press, 7612 Cowan Ave., Los Angeles, CA 90045).
5. Plotinus, *Ennead* I. 6. 8.
6. The Letters of Gerard Manley Hopkins to Robert Bridges. Claude Colleer Abbott, ed. (London: Oxford U. Press, 1935.), p. 137.
7. Rainer Maria Rilke, *Poems from the Book of Hours* (New York: New Directions Press, 1941), p. 31.
8. Rudolph Bultmann, *Theology of the New Testament* (New York: Charles Scribner's Sons, 1951), p. 116.
9. Sören Aabye Kierkegaard, *Either/Or I* (Princeton: Princeton University Press, 1946), p. 237.
10. Dietrich Bonhoeffer, *Christ the Center* (N.Y.: Harper & Row, 1960), p. 61.
11. Dorothy Sayers, *The Whimsical Christian* (New York: Macmillan Co., 1978), p. 168.
12. Martin Buber, *The Knowledge of Man* (N.Y.: Harper & Row, 1965), p. 146.
13. Ibid.

14. Ibid., p. 136.
15. Ibid., p. 157.
16. Stanley Hauerwas, "The Demands of a Truthful Story: Ethics and the Pastoral Task," *Chicago Studies*, Spring 1982, p. 67.
17. Robert Coles, *Walker Percy: An American Search* (Boston: Little Brown & Co., 1978), p. 133.
18. Kierkegaard, *Either/Or I*, p. 22.
19. This method is based on that perfected by Dennis Linn and Matthew Linn, described in their Book *Healing of Memories* (New York: Paulist Press, 1974).
20. James Mackey, *Jesus: Man and the Myth* (New Jersey: Paulist Press, 1979), p. 144.
21. Mary Bosanquet, *The Life and Death of Dietrich Bonhoeffer* (London: Hodder & Stoughton, 1968), p. 270.
22. Psalm 8.
23. Charles Davis, "The Experience of God and the Search for Images," in *Is God God?* (Nashville: Abingdon Press, 1981), p. 50.